BEING THE CHURCH

ROBERT GRIFFITH

Copyright © 2024 Grace and Truth Publishing

All rights reserved. No part of this book may be reproduced, stored in a retrieval system, or transmitted in any form, without the written permission of Grace and Truth Publishing.

GRACE AND TRUTH PUBLISHING
PO Box 338, Gunnedah NSW 2380 Australia
www.graceandtruthpublishing.com.au

All Bible quotes are from the New International Version (NIV) expect where otherwise stated.

NEW INTERNATIONAL VERSION (NIV), Copyright 1973, 1978 and 1984 by international Bible Society. Used by permission of Zondervan Publishing House. All rights reserved.

Other version quotes are from:

AMPLIFIED BIBLE (AMP), Copyright © 1954, 1958, 1962, 1964, 1965, 1987 by The Lockman Foundation. Used by permission.

ENGLISH STANDARD VERSION (ESV), Copyright © 2001 by Crossway Bibles, a division of Good News Publishers. Used by permission. All rights reserved.

NEW AMERICAN STANDARD BIBLE (NASB), Copyright © 1960, 1962, 1963, 1968, 1971, 1972, 1973, 1975, 1977, by The Lockman Foundation. Used by permission.

NEW KING JAMES VERSION (NKJV), Copyright © 1979, 1980, 1982, by Thomas Nelson Inc. Used by permission. All rights reserved.

THE MESSAGE (MSG), by Eugene Peterson, Copyright © 1993, 1994, 1995, 1996, and 2000. Used by permission of NavPress Publishing Group. All rights reserved.

REVISED STANDARD VERSION (RSV), Copyright © 1973, by Thomas Nelson Inc. Used by permission. All rights reserved.

Quotes in square brackets are the author's comment.

ISBN 978-0-648-64390-6

TABLE OF CONTENTS

1	Finding God in Exile	5
2	It's all Greek to Me	12
3	Spectator or Team Member?	20
4	The Church is Not an Institution	30
5	The Church is the Hope of the World	37
6	Worship God	44
7	In His Steps	53
8	Our Partnership with God	59
9	Koinonia Fellowship	68
10	Giving the Church Back to God	76
11	The Weeds of Unbelief	84
12	Come, Holy Spirit	94
13	Hearing from God	114
14	Abiding in Christ	122
15	Walking in the Spirit	132
16	Aligning Ourselves with God	141
17	Embracing our Design	149
18	Loving God	155
19	Christ in our Midst	162
20	The Dwelling Place of God	171

PREFACE

Many years ago, I heard the founder of the Vineyard Church, John Wimber, share his personal testimony. He recalled his first visit to a local congregation after making a commitment to Jesus. He sat through the service and enjoyed the music and the sermon and then the Pastor gave the blessing and it was all over. John was confused. He introduced himself to the Pastor and said he was a new believer and he had one question. *"When do we get to do the stuff?"* The Pastor seemed a little bemused and replied, *"What stuff do you mean?"* John replied, *"The stuff in the book! The stuff the believers did when the Church was born! When do we get to do that stuff?"*

John learned that many congregations don't 'do the stuff' anymore, they just sing about it, read about it and remember the glory days of the church. It was that conversation which planted the seed in Wimber's heart to establish the Vineyard Church and embark upon his extensive international teaching ministry.

I also recall a time early in my Christian pilgrimage when I faced the same dilemma reading the book of Acts and comparing the modern church with the early church. I could not understand how a dynamic, Spirit-led, Christ-centred, relational community could be transformed so radically into what is, more often than not, an event-based, task-centred, rule-governed religion. Or in other cases the church of Jesus Christ has been reduced to a socio-political welfare agency with little or no reference to Christ or the gospel. You simply cannot compare the early church and the modern church without wondering, 'what happened?'

This book is my humble attempt to answer that question and explore the radical difference between 'going to church' (what tends to happen today) and 'being the church' (how it was when all this began). This is a theological issue, a pastoral issue, a social issue and perhaps the most important issue of our time.

Robert Griffith

CHAPTER ONE
Finding God in Exile

There was nothing intrinsically good about the global pandemic which took the world captive in 2020. Over two gruelling years it brought pain, death and economic hardship to almost every country in the world. God did not bring this disaster upon us, but nor was God taken by surprise. He was at work doing what God always does in times of trouble - bringing good from bad, hope from despair and purpose from tragedy. Every cloud has a silver lining when we trust in God and there has been a silver lining to this massive cloud for the church.

Before the pandemic, the global reach of the church and our presence on the internet was moderate, at best. Thousands of congregations had little or no online presence and only engaged with the people who walked in the door of their church building each week. When the pandemic hit us, we saw a huge online explosion of Christian content and the gospel of Jesus Christ was reaching millions more people than it had before.

Most churches were forced to take their worship services and their teaching online so their own people could still connect with each other every week. When that happened these churches effectively opened their doors to the whole world. So many congregations across the globe reported that they were now connecting with a lot more people each week online than they ever had in person before the onset of the pandemic.

In my own congregation at the time, we were connecting with at least six times as many people every week than we had in our congregation. Better still, many of those people remained connected to our online teaching after pandemic passed. Whilst we may have lacked the fullness of the whole church experience for that season because of the absence of face-to-face fellowship, we nevertheless 'enlarged our tents' in ways which should now challenge how we 'do' church in a post-pandemic world. This experience forced many church leaders to face this important question once again: *What does it mean to truly be the church?*

That is the question I will be exploring in this important book. Of course, the best place to start in that exploration is at the beginning. In Acts chapter 2 we have a snapshot of the birth and infancy of the church which Jesus promised to build. There we see what the church looked like before we messed it up! This is how the followers of Christ lived and ministered before that day when the Roman Emperor Constantine dragged us away from our daily worship, our home group meetings, fellowship meals and daily times in prayer, and put us into pagan halls where we held events and gatherings. Over just a few decades, the concept of the church changed, or to be blunt, it was completely lost.

That was two hundred years after Christ walked the earth and that was the point in our history where the spiritual, God-ordained, intrinsic, relational concept of 'being the church' was replaced by a secular, extrinsic, activity-based concept of 'going to church.' What was a 24-hours-a-day, 7-days-a-week lifestyle flowing from a personal relationship with a living, present God through His Spirit, sadly became a series of events and then a place we 'go to' once a week or maybe more if we are really committed.

Of course, all that changed in March 2020 when we were told to stop 'going to church' and most church buildings were closed for an extended period of time. Many believers grieved the loss of those gatherings in our buildings and that's understandable because a lot of very special things happen in those places. When the restrictions were finally lifted, my hope and prayer was that this forced 'exile' would have done its work in our hearts as God reminded us of what it really means to be the church.

Of course, the people of God have been here before. When the Israelites finally returned to Jerusalem in 538BC after their imposed exile in Babylon, they were not the same people (at least for a while anyway). They had been forced to find God in exile, outside their temple, in a foreign land - something they never dreamed of before. My prayer has been that God's people today across the world will have also found God in exile outside our buildings during the pandemic. So, what does it mean to truly _be_ the church?

When the resurrected Christ spoke to His disciples just before leaving this earthly kingdom, He told them to wait. Wait for what? Wait for the promised Holy Spirit. In essence Jesus was saying this:

I have called you, equipped you, taught you and led you these past few years as a man. However, if my kingdom purpose is to be fulfilled across the whole world, I can no longer lead you in this way. I promised I would be with you always – to the ends of the earth - and I will. But that can no longer be in the flesh, it must be in and through the Holy Spirit.

So, on the day we called the day of Pentecost, the Spirit of Christ was released in the hearts of hundreds and then thousands of people and the church as we know it (or should know it) was born. The final verses of Acts chapter 2 clearly show us what this new spirit-led, relational community looked like. That snapshot of the church is found in the final six verses.

They devoted themselves to the apostles' teaching and to fellowship, to the breaking of bread and to prayer. Everyone was filled with awe at the many wonders and signs performed by the apostles. All the believers were together and had everything in common. They sold property and possessions to give to anyone who had need. Every day they continued to meet together in the temple courts. They broke bread in their homes and ate together with glad and sincere hearts, praising God and enjoying the favour of all the people and the Lord added to their number daily those who were being saved. (Acts 2:42-47)

Now I have read those words thousands of times and, after all these years, the hairs still stand up on the back of my neck! I don't know why. Perhaps it's simply because when I see who we once were as the church, I have renewed hope that we could be that community again. I must confess however that as my years in ministry grow in number, that sense of hope can sometimes find itself under attack as bewilderment and despair grow. I'm a 'glass-half-full' kind of person, I am not discouraged easily, but I also have to face the facts.

I have to accept that this amazing portrait of what 'being the church' really looks like has been in our face in the book of Acts for 2,000 years and yet the majority of people who identify as active Christians are still just 'going to church' and wondering why there are less and less people when they get there or why the ones who are there don't live like or worship like people who have been powerfully, gloriously and permanently set free by the living, reigning, present Christ in their hearts and in their midst when they gather.

We are told in Acts 2 that in the church Jesus was building, *"everyone was filled with awe..."* It was indeed a miracle of God. Previously antagonistic, hostile people were brought together in love by the power of the gospel. The sense of anticipation and awe at the movement of God's Spirit among the people was palpable. It was profound. It was tangible. God was manifesting His presence, His power and His Kingdom purposes right in their midst; in their homes; around their dinner tables; on their streets and in the marketplace. They could see the vision and the mission of Christ exploding before their eyes. In fact, they were part of it - every single day. That's what 'being the church' really looks like!

In Proverbs 29:18 (KJV) we read that simple, yet profound truth, *"Where there is no vision, the people perish."* The word *vision* has been given all kinds of meanings in our modern world and most of them have nothing to do with this verse. But when the NIV Bible was written, the translators tried to be more accurate to the original meaning of the text and this verse became, *"Where there is no revelation, the people cast off restraint."* What the King James Version translated 'vision' the NIV translates 'revelation.' For us today, vision can (and most often does) come from us. But revelation comes from God.

Now this is not just an issue about how a verse is translated. This verse, when properly understood, becomes an explanation for nearly all of the church's highs and lows over our entire history. When the daily revelation of God is not continually being sought, discerned and applied, then we 'cast off restraint; we go our own way; tragically thinking it's God's way because we opened our 'vision' meeting in prayer! When the late Eugene Petersen wrote *The Message,* which is a contemporary translation of the Bible, he unpacked this verse even more and made it abundantly clear what it really means for us today. I really love his interpretation of this important statement. It is as clear as it is confronting.

> *If people can't see what God is doing, they stumble all over themselves; But when they attend to what He reveals, they are most blessed. (Proverbs 29:18)*

If the early church had persevered in 'attending to what God was revealing', then they would probably have said 'No thanks,' to Constantine in 313AD when he signed the Edict of Milan and declared that Christianity was now the official religion of Rome. They should have seen through this 'victory' and realized that everything was about the change - and not for the better. They should have remained a loose movement of persecuted pilgrims who worshipped, fellowshipped and ate together in each other's homes, devoting themselves to prayer and what was to become New Testament teaching as they continued to infiltrate every area of society - seven days a week.

If the church was attending to what God was revealing it would not have allowed Rome to dictate how it behaved and operated and the legalism and corruption which eventually strangled the church would not have emerged and there would have been no need for the Reformation over a thousand years later. In fact, I believe you can trace every stumble, every error, every backward step, every loss to the enemy of truth back to the church failing to really see what God was doing. Worse still – not even looking for God at work in the first place!

It's clear that the people mentioned in Acts 2 saw what God was doing and so they didn't stumble for a very long time! They attended to what God was revealing and they were blessed beyond measure. I encourage you to read though the book of Acts in one sitting when you have time and something will be very clear to you: God was running the show! What the disciples of Jesus preached; when they preached; to whom they preached; who they healed and who they didn't heal; what towns they went to and how long they stayed - everything was under the day-by-day direction of God through His Holy Spirit and the more they attended to what God was doing and revealing, the more they grew and God's kingdom exploded across the world.

When we fast forward more than 2,000 years, we see in so many areas of the church how we are stumbling over ourselves and not seeing what God is doing and not hearing what God is saying. But even in that statement there is hope – great hope. In spite of our actions or inaction, God is still speaking to those who have ears to hear. God is still revealing to those who have eyes to see. God is still active and moving among us and fulfilling His purposes. God has never left us – no matter how wrong we get it or how often we do it our way and not His way – He never goes away and He never stops speaking. We just stop listening, or sadder still, some of us may never have even started listening and have no real expectation of God speaking to us.

For many years now I have encouraged people to ask two questions every morning as their feet hit the floor and they begin each new day. *"What are You doing, Lord?"* and *"How can I be part of it today?"* That's what I've been trying to do my entire ministry and I believe these questions remind us of who we are and also Whose we are. The more we ask those questions and learn to discern the voice of God – the more we will see the difference between 'going to church' and 'being the church.'

It is my prayer that the Spirit of God will lead us all to the point where we stop going to church! Yes, that's right, I want you to stop 'going to church.' The term itself is grammatical nonsense and theological heresy. We don't 'go to' church. We <u>are</u> the church and we need to learn once more how to truly <u>be</u> the church. There were thousands of signs in front of church buildings across the world during the recent pandemic which read something like, *"Our building is closed, but our church is still open!"* Saying that is easy - living that is the challenge we all face every day.

So, as you work your way through this book, I want to make a bold promise to you: If you truly open your mind and heart and intentionally engage with the teaching here, not just gloss over it and receive at a cerebral level, I can guarantee that you will be transformed by God into who He has called you to be. If we can all do that, then the church which Jesus promised to build will be seen in all her glory as we let go of the church we have been struggling to build in Jesus' name. Trust me when I say that you will be amazed at what God can achieve through you and the believers around you when you decide you want to stop just going to church and start being the church!

We need to work with God here and actively look for His hand at work and listen for His voice. This teaching needs to be studied and prayed through - not just read once and discarded. I would strongly suggest when you have made your way to the end of this book that you go back and work through each chapter again in prayer, asking God to reveal His word to you today.

If you choose to spend that time and let God really drive His Word home in your heart, then I can guarantee that 'being the church' will not be a chore, an expectation or a religious activity - it will be a spontaneous reality as the life of Christ explodes within you. Then, before we know it, the book of Acts will no longer be a dusty historical account of where this all began, it will once again be a commentary on where we are now, and who we are becoming as we give the church back to God and the ministry back to His people. Then we can watch Him do today and tomorrow, what He did back then.

That is the reason I preach and write – I want to lead people to the God Who still speaks, still heals, still transforms lives and whole communities. Everything I do, say, write, preach and pray is directed towards that end. I truly believe God is always ready to redeem what we've lost and give us the only thing we ever truly needed: Jesus – the living, present, Lord of the church and the One Who promised to build His church, right here, right now, if we let go the reigns and trust Him. Let those who have ears to hear, listen to what the Spirit of God is saying to us today.

CHAPTER TWO
It's all Greek to Me

When I encouraged you in the previous chapter to stop 'going to' church and start 'being' the church, I was not suggesting we stop gathering together. In fact, the more we understand what being the church really means, then the more important our gatherings will become. What needs to change is our perspective and our understanding of where these gatherings belong in the much larger picture of the church. Some have suggested that it needed a global pandemic and the forced closure of all our church buildings for an extended period of time before we started to seriously explore what being the church really means. Perhaps that is true. Only time will tell.

Of course, the church is not where we go or what we do - the church is who we are. We will never change the world by going to church, but we can certainly change the world by being the church. In fact, that is our calling, our purpose and the reason the church exists. As we saw in the last chapter, in the closing verses of Acts chapter 2 we have a snapshot of what the church first looked like, and we will be looking more closely at those verses in this book because they are foundational. However, I want us to understand something even more foundational first.

If we want to embrace what 'being the church' really means then we have to understand what the church is (or is supposed to be) and what the church is not. There is a lot to learn about the church, but sadly, there are some things we need to <u>unlearn</u> as well. Where do we go to discover the truth about the true church which Jesus established and has been building all these years? The Bible? Of course, that's where we go, however, on this issue, that presents us with a significant problem and what I am about to share with you is really important.

What is the oldest English Bible Translation we have in the modern era? The King James Translation. Do you know when it was written? It was written over a seven-year period and was completed in 1611. Then for over 350 years this was the Bible used by the English-speaking world and today there are still many Christians who use this translation.

Now we need to understand that the church had changed a lot before this translation was even published. As I've mentioned before, the church we encounter in the book of Acts changed dramatically less than 300 years after it was formed. In February 313AD, Christianity was declared the official religion of Rome and Emperor Constantine signed the infamous Edict of Milan.

At that point everything changed. Within a few short years the followers of Jesus were no longer meeting in homes and spreading the gospel through a network of relationships and house churches. They were now all part of a State-sanctioned institution and the entire ministry of the Kingdom of God soon centred around gatherings in buildings each Sunday and that's the way it stayed.

So, when a group of men (there were no women) sat around a table 1,500 years later debating the meaning of the Hebrew and Greek text as they translated the Scriptures into English, the church was already very different and they had centuries of tradition flowing through their veins and influencing their minds. That partially explains what I am about to tell you. Before we examine what we think the Bible says about the church we need to understand something which, for some of us may be confronting, but it's really important. The term 'church' is not actually in the original Greek text.

When the translators of the King James Bible inserted the term 'church' in many places, they were actually in error. They broke some of the most basic and important rules of translation as they allowed their experience and understanding of <u>what the church had become</u>, to influence their description of <u>how the church really was</u> in the beginning and still should be today. This error brought significant consequences for everyone reading the Bible from that time to the present day. They actually presented an alternative picture to what God originally had in mind for the Body of Christ. Poorly translated text, changed the very nature of the church as we should understand it.

Before I go any further, I want to stress that I am not anti-anything and nor am I starting any revolutions or talking about conspiracy theories or undermining the authority of Scripture. Quite the opposite, in fact. Critically analysing translations is really important if we want to be true to the original authors and hearers of the Scriptures. I'm sure that all of us want to see the church of Jesus Christ fulfill the kingdom purposes of God and to see every disciple of Christ reach their potential and be part of the mission of Christ on earth. There is no higher calling.

Quite clearly, that is not happening right now. Look around; read the news; examine the world in which we live. You don't need to be a scholar or theologian to work that out. The followers of Jesus, whom we call the church, don't seem to be making much of a dent in the rapid secularization of society and the spread of evil. Something obviously must change. Something that's wrong needs to be made right. Something that's missing needs to be found. Something that's holding us back needs to be removed. Perhaps all of the above!

The first thing that needs to change is our understanding of the word 'church' in the Bible. The King James translation uses the word 'church' 112 times, having translated the Greek word *ecclesia* to mean church. But let's look at the actual word church in our language. The word comes from the Old English and German word pronounced *kirche*. In Scotland and Northern England it was *kirk* and it referred to what we think of as church.

In earlier Greek it was pronounced *ku-ri-a-kos* or *ku-ri-a-kon*. This is a word that doesn't even remotely resemble the Greek word *ecclesia* which has been translated church in almost all places. Now the meaning of *ku-ri-a-kos* is understood by its root, *ku- ri-os*, which means lord. Therefore, *kuriakos* (i.e. 'church') means 'pertaining to a lord.' It refers to something that pertains to, or belongs to, a lord.

Therfore, the word *church* would have been an acceptable translation for the Greek word *kuriakos*. But the translators inserted the word *church* in the English versions, even though they were not translating the Greek word *kuriakos*. The word they were supposed to be translating was *ecclesia*. Now even the most liberal translator today would never regard *church* as an acceptable translation for the Greek word *ecclesia*. It's an entirely different word with an entirely different meaning than *kuriakos*.

The Greek word *kuriakos* actually only appears in the New Testament twice. Firstly in 1 Corinthians 11:20 where it refers to 'the Lord's supper,' and once again in Revelation 1:10 where it speaks of 'the Lord's day.' In both of those cases, it is translated *the Lord's* - not *church*. Even though the word does not appear again in the New Testament the word *church* as it has come to be known in the English language has replaced *ecclesia*. Does any of this really make a difference? Yes, it does - if we really want our understanding of the church of Jesus Christ to be what Matthew, Luke, Peter, John and Paul envisioned when they each referred to what we think of as *church*.

Let's unpack this some more by first looking at the correct meaning of the word, *ecclesia*. This Greek word is found in the New Testament approximately 115 times, and that's just in this one grammatical form. It appears also in other forms. There are three exceptions in the King James translation where it is properly translated. They are found in Acts 19:32, 39, 41. Here the translators used the word *assembly* instead of church. But the Greek word is exactly the same as the other 112 entries where *church* was used. In Acts 19, *ecclesia* is a town council, a civil body of people gathering together in Ephesus.

So, you can see that *church* wouldn't work there as they had nothing to do with gathering as a body of believers in Christ. And yet still in 112 other places the translators used the word *church* when translating *ecclesia*. Quite simply, that should never have happened. The Greek word *ecclesia* is correctly defined as 'the called-out (ones)' The term 'ecc' in Greek means 'out' and 'kaleo' means 'call.' So, what do we think the writers of the New Testament meant when they used the word *ecclesia* to describe the followers of Jesus?

Well, we already know that many Christian words we use today already existed before Christ and were just given a new meaning when the church was born. For example, the Greek word *euaggelion* is translated *gospel* and meant a *proclamation*. But the New Testament writers used that word to talk specifically about the gospel of Jesus Christ. When they chose the word *ecclesia* to describe this new community which came into being on the Day of Pentecost, what did they mean? They obviously meant a community of believers in Christ summoned by God and called out (by Him) from among the Jewish and Roman peoples to come together into a separate community under His Lordship - an autonomous body of believers under the Kingship of Jesus Christ. They would bow to no other king but Jesus. They would obey the rules of the nation so long as they did not conflict with their obedience to their King. They would serve no one but the Lord.

That's why these same believers often ran into trouble with the rulers of the day, whether it be the Sanhedrin or later kings and rulers. They were arrested, crucified and martyred because they served only King Jesus and not Caesar. This would have been seen as a declaration of war or treason. Such is the way of the 'called out ones' - such is the true church. Those who came to the Lord had to understand that they were making a serious choice. But they valued an eternity with the Lord over whatever it would cost them in this life.

Paul and Silas were therefore not 'church planters' as so many have called them. These men were Kingdom builders! They were not advocating that people find a place to be separate and not influence anyone around them, meeting for a few hours on the weekend, singing a few songs, hearing a sermon and then going home. Paul and others taught the principles of a theocracy where God alone ruled as benevolent but holy Sovereign and of family values and the standards of justice and equality, all of which God gave to Israel through Moses.

This was now the work of the Almighty one-and-only God Whom they would obey at all costs, even unto death, as their hearts responded to the call to become citizens of Christ's eternal Kingdom and join themselves to the *ecclesia* or community of believers who were 'called out' of the political and cultural status quo to serve the King of Kings and Lord of Lords.

We therefore see that the idea of the church as a group of people meeting in a specific location (or building) as believers doesn't even come close to what the New Testament writers were thinking or living! Neither did it have anything to do with denominations where one group believed this but not that, keeping their distance from their fellow believers based on those differences. It would have been heresy to even consider such divisions in the early church. They were one in Christ - there was no other reality. If divisions arose, they sorted them out with firm, Godly leadership under the guidance of the Holy Spirit.

Jesus Christ sent the believers into the world just as His Father had sent Him. Therefore, it would not be surprising that He told His disciples *"If the world hates you, keep in mind that it hated me first.* (John 15:18). Now you can see why that would be the case. Jesus came against the ungodly leadership that was functioning in the temple - men who had their own political agendas and power to protect.

When you consider that the early believers for well over 200 years met in homes and were free in their associations with one another, we can see that to have their identity so connected with what takes place in a specific building where most of the 'church business' takes place today, would enormously hinder their interaction with and identity within the community around them.

As you may already know, the buildings that were instituted by the State and set up by Emperor Constantine in 325 A.D. changed everything. Not that buildings are bad. They provide a place for meeting, just as homes do. The buildings themselves are not the real issue, then or now. The problem is the whole idea of 'attending church' with its rather predictable agenda as part of a non-interactive audience. That is what sucked the life out of the Body of Christ. Such a concept of church cannot be compared to the dynamic, spontaneous, passionate commitment to God and each other in the fellowship of 'the called-out ones' who know they have been summoned by God to come out of the prevailing society into His Kingdom. History records that time and again they valued this calling more than their own lives.

Let me then ask you: do you think God might want to make some changes in the church we see today before Christ returns? Is it possible that the mission of Christ cannot be fulfilled until we stop *going to* church and start *being* the church? Now before you shout 'amen' too quickly, be warned, this is not going to be easy. The real church I have just described isn't something we can simply say, *"OK then, let's be like that."* It will take an internal work of the Holy Spirit, just as it did for the early believers. Our job is to love the Lord with all our heart, soul, mind and strength, love each other with the love of Christ, and be available for God to speak to us, move in us and build that true church, against which the gates of hell itself will not prevail. That may mean a complete re-think on our part concerning who we are and what being the church really means for us.

We live in exciting times. God is on the move. His Spirit is stirring in so many congregations across the world, both large and small, young and old. He is re-introducing His children to their roots. What I have been preaching for many years now is part of the wider matrix of what God is doing elsewhere also. Have we messed up? Yes, we have. Have we gotten it wrong more than we've gotten it right? Of course we have. Have we missed the essence of the New Testament view of the church by not translating the original text well or not reading it with the Holy Spirit by our side? Most definitely. Can God fix all that and still fulfill His kingdom plan and purpose in us and through us? Absolutely!

When Jesus told His disciples about the coming of the Holy Spirit, He promised that *"the Spirit will guide you into all truth."* (John 16:13). That is exactly what the Holy Spirit will do, if we let Him. It doesn't matter how many times we get it wrong; we only have to get it right once to see God do immeasurably more than all we ask or even imagine. That is His promise!

I want to assure you that 'being the church' is not especially complicated. It's not a mountain we can't climb or a river we can't cross. We have exhausted ourselves over many centuries now trying to grow the church and build an institution – neither of which God ever called us to do!

God called us to BE. More specifically, God called us to be <u>His</u>. The rest is God's responsibility. Jesus Christ will build His church; it was never our job. Jesus will advance His kingdom on earth as it is in heaven – we cannot do that – we can only pray for that. Our job is to make choices which are consistent with what the church is meant to be and let God do the rest.

Evangelism is not a task we are given to do – evangelism is the natural outflow of a healthy church. It is God Who adds to our number daily those who are being saved (Acts 2:47). Our job is to witness to the reality of Christ in us and then disciple those whom God awakens and draws into His eternal Kingdom.

In this book I will <u>not</u> be giving you a list of things to <u>do</u> in order to be the church. In fact, we may well discover a list of things we need to stop doing and stop believing! Because one of the greatest enemies of 'being' is 'doing' and our western culture has conditioned us from birth to do, do, do, do! God wants to change that, and if we let Him, then we will at last see the church as it was meant to be.

Before turning this page and continuing this important equipping journey, I want to encourage you to meditate upon this simple, yet profound verse for a day or so and let the Spirit of God grip your heart with its simplicity, but also its critical importance for the church today.

If people can't see what God is doing, they stumble all over themselves; But when they attend to what He reveals, they are most blessed. (Proverbs 29:18 MSG)

CHAPTER THREE
Spectator or Team Member?

Within thirty years of Christ's ascension, the gospel was being preached in every single outpost of the Roman Empire. It was unencumbered by mortgages, committees, staff salaries and conflicts between choir rehearsal and the church cricket team practice. These 'followers of the Way' blazed a trail of stunning success across many nations. The growth of this new community of faith was phenomenal. As the church of Jesus Christ exploded in those first few centuries, it thrived in hard times and endured dreadful persecution.

The early church had so much going for them, but there were three strengths which stood out. The first was the observable presence of the living God in their hearts and in their midst. Secondly, the gatherings of the church were an informal and often-boisterous affair with a full meal, not just a polite ceremony with a scrap of bread and a thimbleful of juice. Church life was a floating celebration, a non-stop progressive dinner as everyone ate at each other's houses and all participated in the various festivities. Thirdly, when the believers came together as the church, everyone was the star of the show, everyone was needed. Spirits were lifted; problems were solved; hurts were healed; hearts were fed; and the Lord of Lords spoke to every soul. But the most outrageous part of the meeting was definitely the 'love-feast' (Jude 12), which resembled a cross between a grand final victory celebration and a New Year's Eve party!

From our vantage point today, it looks as if they had an unbeatable thing going. A sure-fire, runaway, free-wheeling style of church that was gobbling up Satan's territory like a giant pacman and expanding in size and impact at an unbelievable pace. So, what on earth happened? Why did that roaring success in the early years of the church fade? When did we cool off? At what point did the wheels fall off this incredible glory train? What caused everything about the church to change so radically, so comprehensively, and with such tragic outcomes?

As the church grew larger and more popular, our feeling of being a distinct family waned. The church became less of the dynamic revolutionary band it once was and become a static establishment. It changed from being an organic, Spirit-led, transformational movement and became a human organisation. The final straw came in AD 313, when Emperor Constantine signed the Edict of Milan, officially 'tolerating' the church and ending years of persecution. Church leaders from popes to local bishops got involved with the government. Many even became officials. At that time, it looked like a good idea. (*"Hey guys, we won! Now we can take over!"*).

However, as it turned out, it was a really, really bad idea. Our top leaders drifted away on a long power trip and let their flocks scatter. Before long, we ceased being an interactive family; that dynamic, well-equipped army we were called to be - and we soon became an audience. Team members became spectators of an elite few who were given 'up front' roles. The biggest blunder of all came when the church began constructing buildings which would become their new 'home.' No more meetings in the catacombs and forest glens and no more warm get togethers in someone's living room or out under the oak tree.

Modelled after the Roman pagan forums, the new buildings now held hundreds of Christians - all sitting in rows looking towards a podium and platform where the important people were now speaking. Of course, you can no longer have intimate, easy interaction with that size crowd and in that setting. From day one, these new 'sanctuaries' put limits on free expression. It was not long before the new crib ended up strangling the baby.

Imagine if you were living in that time: You may have felt at ease confessing a sin to a couple dozen friends in Joseph's and Elizabeth's living room - but in front of five hundred strangers? No way! If God taught you something during the week and it lay strongly on your heart, you wouldn't hesitate to stand up and spend ten minutes sharing it in Joe and Betty's back room. But here in this fancy new hall, with hundreds present, there are probably at least fifty people with a message burning in their hearts. So, it was a case of take a number!

Also, over at Joe and Betty's place, everybody got into the act in the worship time. You were able to praise the Lord from your heart - again and again as you felt led by the Spirit. It was the most meaningful and healing moment of your week. But here? Not likely – only the really good speakers, singers and musicians were now given that opportunity. Without modern acoustics or roving microphones, large open meetings with so many people became difficult. So closed meetings took over. Gradually the speaking became centralized in a pulpit and order was firmly maintained. (Again, it seemed like a good idea at the time.) Back at Joe and Betty's, you were an active participant; here, you are a spectator - a passive listener – just a face in the crowd.

At first you don't mind it - the change is exciting and being with 500 believers at once feels like paradise! Time marches on and now, with 1,000 eyes focused on the pulpit, the man behind it has become extremely important. He's very good, of course - probably the best speaker in the area. His warmth and wisdom and skill defuse any latent objections to this new state of affairs. Certainly, his polished sermons beat the sandals off all those impromptu teachings you used to hear - and give - at Joe and Betty's place. So, it doesn't take long before every local church from London to Alexandria has its own building and its own professional Christian standing up the front every Sunday, doing all the talking. Eventually, the love-feasts got so big and rowdy they were banned. Everything changed – and radically.

Yet we see no prophet or Godly leader raising their voice, mourning the passing of the house church or condemning the new diversion of church funds into real estate development. Nobody of any importance questions taking initiative away from ordinary believers and bestowing it upon a new priesthood class; nobody dared point out that the teaching of Jesus and the Apostles never sanctioned any of this and nor does this look anything like the church Jesus Christ birthed.

Meeting in larger numbers in a purpose-built sanctuary was not a great problem in itself – if this was an innovative addition to all that was happening in the church it might have been a really positive development. But it wasn't an addition at all – it actually replaced most of what the church used to do and be. House churches, shared fellowship over a meal and every-member-ministry – was all gone. Everything which defined the church was replaced with these new centralised meetings.

By A.D. 400, just 87 years later, the Roman Empire had gone from being less than four per cent Christian to eighty per cent Christian ... but with almost no conversions! The government simply decreed that everyone was now a Christian. Evangelism virtually disappeared from the face of the earth during that time.

Think about this. The life-changing, nation-transforming power of the Gospel of Jesus Christ did not regenerate the hearts of these new Christians; they just became Christians because their government declared them to be so. The power and reality behind that phenomenal growth in the early years of the church was now a distance memory!

It was arguably the worst disaster to hit the earth since Noah and the flood! In fact, I believe all the major problems of the church today (other than sin) can be traced back 1,700 years or so, to when the church became an audience. When we switched from living rooms to church buildings and professionally staffed the local church, we lost all our momentum. When people were declared 'Christian' without being transformed by the power of the gospel, the local church became weak, cold and ineffective.

Non-priests were now labelled as 'lay people' a term which is not even found in the Bible - for good reason. As a lay person in a fourth century church building, you no longer approached God directly. The priest did that now on your behalf. Thus, an architectural decision turned into a serious doctrinal problem. The priesthood of all believers was forgotten or ignored and the church began to die from within.

The Bible was only interpreted and read by the priests. This was a logical step - after all, if you're not allowed to decide what it means, why bother reading it? With the Scriptures kept at arm's length from the people, the priesthood was free to play with it unencumbered by the corrective discipline of the whole church community.

For a thousand years, cloistered monks lovingly piled so much theological baggage on top of the Bible until, by the time of Martin Luther, hardly a lay person in Europe could even begin to tell you what 'justification by grace, through faith' meant or why it was so important.

Without the Scriptures to lift them out of the darkness, lay people turned into serfs in the feudalism of the Dark Ages. Ironically, in that darkness the only candle of hope and upward mobility was the church. Becoming a priest was the only way out of oblivion. The medieval church is often praised for providing this sole escape hatch from the pit, whilst we conveniently forgot that the church helped dig that pit in the first place!

The early church had so much success and momentum that they logically should have evangelised everyone from Turkey to Tokyo by A.D. 600. But that didn't happen. What went wrong? As I said, the church got so big and popular that it decided to follow the pagan way and erect its own buildings. This solved a long-standing problem that was actually never a problem in the first place! Whenever a healthy house-church got too big for its living room, it had to split - into two living rooms – then three – then four. New leadership was thus always being trained and raised up to meet the growing needs of this organic, grassroots, rapidly multiplying church.

When church buildings began to sprout across the Empire, Christians no longer had to face the awkward anguish of who got to stay with the favourite elders and who had to split off with the new leaders. Everybody stayed with everybody. It was heavenly ... or was it?

The trouble is, sharing, intimacy and one-on-one ministry were impossible in a crowd of hundreds of people and the bigger the crowd the higher the importance of eloquence for those who spoke or sang or played an instrument. Those stuttering new converts now stayed in their shells. Anonymity soon replaced fellowship. Communication during meetings began to be dominated by the few who could read and had access to books: which, in the end, meant the priests. The laity, citizens of a long-crumbling Roman empire, were turned into spiritual eunuchs and lost the strength the empire needed so desperately at that time. By A.D. 476, Rome fell for the final time and the church led the way into the Dark Ages.

Now a thousand tear-stained years later, Martin Luther, John Calvin and Huldrych Zwingli began picking up the pieces in what we call the Protestant Reformation. They put Christian theology back together like a jigsaw puzzle. They also worked a bit on the church's practices and functions, and got about half of them glued back together, more or less. Fabulous work - the best fix-it job since Nehemiah! But they couldn't do everything. Rome wasn't built in a day and nor was it unbuilt in a day.

So, the Puritans had to pick up some more pieces. In the 18th Century, the Wesleys picked up some more. In the 19th Century, the revivalists and missionaries picked up more. Early in the 20th century, the Pentecostal movement picked up even more. But more reform was needed and so there's still a gigantic hole in the church. The 'priesthood of all believers' - the central goal of the Reformation - has only been restored theologically – it has a long way to go practically. It still exists mainly as a concept.

In very important ways, our churches remain the way they were after Constantine declared Christianity the official religion of Rome and then dictated how that religion would operate. Between clergy and laity there is still a big, un-crossable gap - academic, professional, and liturgical. Lay people today have regained the Word of God, but not necessarily the work of God. The priesthood of all believers has been restored in theory more than in practice.

The very earliest Christians had problems, but the clergy-centred church was not one of them. Their churches were elder-led, and the burden of God's work was spread across all believers like dew on a paddock. Everyone was a minister of the gospel and everyone was equipped to advance the kingdom of heaven by God's grace and for God's glory. There were no spectators – only team members.

The New Testament only makes sense within the context of the early church. So many of the exhortations we have in the

New Testament only make sense when the church looks like and functions like the church Jesus birthed and the Spirit empowered to change the whole world. Let's look at just a few of those exhortations and allow me to emphasise some words here.

> *Now to each one the manifestation of the Spirit is given for the common good. (1 Corinthians 12:7)*
>
> *We have different gifts, according to the grace given to each of us. If your gift is prophesying, then prophesy in accordance with your[a] faith; if it is serving, then serve; if it is teaching, then teach; if it is to encourage, then give encouragement; if it is giving, then give generously; if it is to lead, do it diligently; if it is to show mercy, do it cheerfully. (Romans 12:6-8)*
>
> *To one there is given through the Spirit a message of wisdom, to another a message of knowledge by means of the same Spirit, to another faith by the same Spirit, to another gifts of healing by that one Spirit, to another miraculous powers, to another prophecy, to another distinguishing between spirits, to another speaking in different kinds of tongues and to still another the interpretation of tongues. All these are the work of one and the same Spirit, and he distributes them to each one, just as he determines. (1 Corinthians 12:8-11)*
>
> *But to each one of us grace has been given as Christ apportioned it. (Ephesians 4:7)*
>
> *What then shall we say, brothers and sisters? When you come together, each of you has a hymn, or a word of instruction, a revelation, a tongue or an interpretation. Everything must be done so that the church may be built up." (1 Corinthians 14:26)*
>
> *So Christ himself gave the apostles, the prophets, the evangelists, the pastors and teachers, to equip his people for works of service, so that the body of Christ may be built up until we all reach unity in the faith and in the knowledge of the Son of God and become mature, attaining to the whole measure of the fullness of Christ.*

Then we will no longer be infants, tossed back and forth by the waves, and blown here and there by every wind of teaching and by the cunning and craftiness of people in their deceitful scheming. Instead, speaking the truth in love, we will grow to become in every respect the mature body of him who is the head, that is, Christ. From him the whole body, joined and held together by every supporting ligament, grows and builds itself up in love, as each part does its work. (Ephesians 4:11-16)

Now may the God of peace, who through the blood of the eternal covenant brought back from the dead our Lord Jesus, that great Shepherd of the sheep, equip you with everything good for doing his will, and may he work in us what is pleasing to him, through Jesus Christ, to whom be glory for ever and ever. Amen. (Hebrews 13:20-21)

Just from those seven New Testament excerpts (there are many, many more), we can see that God's intention was that every disciple would become a spirit-filled, spirit-led, fully equipped minister of the gospel, exercising their specific gifts as God had intended. There were no spectators – only team members.

There was no 'clergy' and 'laity' – only disciples operating within their calling and gifting. Yes, there were leaders and overseers, teachers and pastors, but they were never elevated above those they led. They led alongside them. There were no separated, elevated coaches, only player-coaches.

No doubt you've heard the old saying, *'Those who can, do and those who can't, teach.'* It is a derogatory dig at those in leadership who have separated themselves from the 'real people' on the ground and in the front line of the battle. In the New Testament church, that was never the case because those who taught were also those in the front line of ministry, side by side with the ones they were called to nurture, teach and equip.

Every disciple of Jesus Christ was expected to grow up into Christ and be equipped with everything they needed to do God's will. Some of those gifts were leadership gifts, but there were many, many more gifts bestowed upon the people and each and every one of them were needed to work in harmony with each other. The further we drift from the New Testament model, the more impotent, irrelevant and ineffective the church becomes.

Right now, there are millions of Christians around the world praying for revival and for the kingdom of God to rise up and overcome the kingdom of this world. But when asked how that is going to happen, most believers say they don't really know and that such things are in God's hands. What utter balderdash! Read those seven New Testament passages above once more as God makes it abundantly (and embarrassingly) clear that He has chosen us, His people, to achieve His will and fulfill the mission of Christ. In fact, you can go all the way back to 2 Chronicles and read a promise from God which still stands today:

> *If my people, who are called by my name, will humble themselves and pray and seek my face and turn from their wicked ways, then I will hear from heaven, and I will forgive their sin and will heal their land. (2 Chronicles 7:14)*

In our context today, God is effectively saying,

> *If my people, whom I have called and empowered to fulfil My mission on earth, will recognise their calling, accept their gifting, and receive the equipping I give them along the way, then they will see revival, then they will see the wonder, the beauty, the power and the effectiveness of the Body of Christ as My church transforms the world in which they live.*

As God has reminded me again here of my calling, my purpose and my assignment within His kingdom, I really want to give Him the chance to do the same for you as you join me in this equipping journey in the coming chapters. I will explore many different issues and ministry priorities and discover some real keys to advancing God's kingdom on earth. When the church is functioning as it was meant to; when every member accepts their role in the Body of Christ; when each disciple of Jesus exercises their gifts, no matter how large or small they might seem – then the result is as dynamic and amazing as the video I want to tell you about now.

A number of years ago as I was preparing to preach to a combined churches service in my local area, I came across a brief video which had a profound and even prophetic impact on me. The video itself is great and millions of people have enjoyed it over the years. However, I doubt that many of them saw what I saw that day.

When I finished watching this clip for the first time, I felt tears rolling down my cheeks and my heart was beating so powerfully in my chest I thought it would burst. What I saw and heard was amazing in itself – but something much deeper was happening in me that day. I heard that unmistakable voice of God's Spirit saying:

> *That is a picture of the church which I am building and when everyone fulfils their calling and exercises the gifts I have given the church through them - together as one harmonious orchestra - the impact will be even greater than what you have just seen and heard and more overwhelming than what you are feeling now!*

There are many analogies of the church: a family, an army, a hospital, a body. One of the most powerful pictures of the church in action is that of an orchestra and that's the image of the church I want you to focus on when you watch this video and don't just enjoy what you see and hear – look and listen for the prophetic declaration of God as He shows you the power and the beauty and the impact of a fully alive, fully engaged, fully united and fully equipped church.

On your phone, tablet or computer, type the link below into your internet browser and crank up the sound. Then imagine how sweet the sight and sound will be to God, of a fully functioning church where every one of His precious children is playing their part and producing the most amazing, united result!

LINK: https://robertgriffith.net/files/harmony.mp4

CHAPTER FOUR
The Church is not an Institution

Several years ago, I read a quote from Pope Francis from one of his sermons at the Vatican. I am sure there would be many things the Pope and I would strongly disagree on; however, this one statement is not one of them. He was preaching about the church and he made this simple statement: *"The church is a love story, not an institution."* That quote caught my attention not only because it's a beautiful and accurate description, but because it came from the leader of the most institutionalized part of the Christian church. However, it's a quote that sits well with Pope Francis who has been pushing against the confines, rules and practices of that institution throughout his whole life.

Of course, even though we often speak of the 'institutional church,' we need to remember that this is not the language of Scripture and it is a concept which would have been completely foreign, if not abhorrent, to those first Christians all those years ago. The early church and the New Testament both focus on the relationships which lie at the heart of this community of faith we call the church.

In his letter to the Ephesians Paul talks about the church as the 'Body of Christ', the 'Household of God' and the 'Family of God.' Peter refers to the church as the 'Flock of God' and the 'People of God' and in Revelation, John says the church is the 'Bride of Christ.' In Scripture, the church is always depicted in terms of relationships. Relationships lie at the very heart of the church. These relationships are based on love because God is love. So, the church is the 2,000-year-old ongoing love story about God and His redeemed. In fact, the church only succeeds to the extent that we respond in love to the love of God in Christ.

So let me ask you a personal question. Do you love Jesus? More importantly, do you know how much you are loved by Jesus? As a Christian are you caught up in this amazing love story? Your 'husband,' your 'bridegroom' sacrificed everything for you but do you live in the light of that love every day? Pardon me if this sounds like mushy nonsense, but it actually speaks to the very essence of being the church.

Can you remember one of the last conversations Jesus had with His close friend Peter? It was after Jesus had risen from the dead and He was on the beach one morning and He asked Peter a question. In fact, He asked him three times in a row – just to make sure Peter understood. Jesus asked Peter, *"Do you love me?"* I find this fascinating. Here is Peter, upon whose confession Jesus said earlier He was going to build His church. This is one of Jesus' last encounters with Peter before leaving forever in the flesh. I imagine Jesus could have asked Peter lots of questions at this vital moment. Questions like, *"Are you ready to lead these people? Do you remember what I taught you about making disciples? Do you know how to deal with those who come against you?"* I could think of a hundred important questions for a moment like this. But the only thing which Jesus thought was important to ask Peter before leaving was a question about their relationship and He asked it three times: *"Peter, do you love me?"*

Our love relationship with Christ lies at the very heart of our identity as His followers, His disciples and the church which bears His name. Everything begins and ends right here as we look Jesus in the eye and respond when He asks us, *"Do you love me?"* The church is a not a gathering of people in a particular place or under a particular banner. It is most certainly not a group of people who subscribe to a particular doctrine – that's religion and God hates religion. That's what the Pharisees had established when Jesus arrived and He blew all that out of the water entirely with His radical message of love and grace.

I truly love the church Jesus is building from the depths of my heart, but I have no affection whatsoever for the institution mankind has tried so hard to build. I genuinely love the church; the community of God's people; the 'called out' ones who love Jesus and are committed to His ongoing mission on earth. I love the men, women, and young people with whom I have been able to share my life, worship and serve alongside in the name of Jesus.

For decades now we've heard the adage, *"the church isn't the building, it's the people."* But do we really believe that? Most of us recognize that the bricks and mortar structure isn't the church, but somehow, we haven't had the same epiphany about the intangible structures, programs, regulations and activities of that institution. Whether we know it or not, in the imagination of most people, the Christian church is a collection of programs, committees, policies, teams, ministries, initiatives, budgets and events. Most people speak of 'the church' the same way they speak of 'the government' - it's an organization with a hierarchy of leaders managing a structured program of activities.

I see this dichotomy most clearly when it comes to volunteer service. As church leaders we often feel compelled to draw more people into the institution's programs to serve. Pastors and leaders scan the membership directory and mark all the possible recruits who are not presently 'serving the church.' But where did we find such a concept? It most certainly was not in the New Testament – upon which we claim to base our entire lives and ministry. We have never been called to serve the church. Even the now common labels we use for people such as the 'churched' or the 'unchurched' testifies to the centrality of the institution in our minds and in our mission.

The whole 'church growth' movement we experienced in the last couple decades of the twentieth century cemented this institutional mindset. When attendance at a church gathering or activity is really large, we say, *"the church is growing,"* when the attendance is quite low we say, *"the church is failing."* But is that accurate? Is the real church, the Body of Christ, the 'called out' ones who love Jesus, really growing or failing, or are we simply observing the rise or fall in size of a man-made institution? Can we even tell the difference anymore?

I know of some large churches with a really poor level of theological and relational maturity. All they really have is an attractive, successful program – not a healthy church. I know of some pretty small and insignificant churches whose members have really grown in their faith and their understanding of the priority of relationships and the centrality of the Holy Spirit in all their activities and they are committed to the mission of Christ. Those people are far closer to the heart of the church which Jesus promised to build and yet, they may be seen as small, insignificant or a failure in the eyes of those who focus on the institution.

Please understand that I am certainly not anti-institution. I believe that some structure is good and at times it may even be God-ordained. We see evidence of a lose structure from the very foundation of the church in Acts. But these structures always existed to serve the mission of Christ and they were always flexible and able to move and grow and adapt as the Holy Spirit led the people of God on a daily basis.

Our structures must always serve the mission of Christ and be subject to the Holy Spirit.

Today, it can at times seem like God's people exist to serve the structures in the fulfilment of the mission of the institution of which they are a part. More often than not, that mission is simply to become a much bigger institution!

I truly believe the number of people who love the church but not the institution has been steadily growing for a number of years now. There's an increasing dissatisfaction among mature believers towards the institution. I don't believe they're rejecting the church like some people say they are. Studies show that these believers continue to grow spiritually by serving God and others and by developing meaningful relationships. In other words, they are growing by engaging with the real church – which consists of people, not programs; relationships not religion. That is the church which Jesus is building and hat is the church the world desperately needs.

I am certainly not advocating we dismantle the institution and I am not suggesting that anyone should leave. Sadly, that's a choice thousands of sincere Christians are making every day across the world – but that's the easy way out and I sincerely believe that is not what God is calling us to do. I pray that those people will reconsider and take the hard road and return to us so they can be part of the new day which is dawning.

It has taken me many years to work through this and it has been a real struggle at times. It even required me to step out of pastoral ministry completely for six years. I had no commitment to return. I called it a sabbatical, but it could just as easily have been a permanent departure from the institution I had been part of for most of my life. Before I returned, I really needed God to make it clear to me that the institution we wrongly call 'church' is not beyond reform. I needed to know it is not beyond hope. I needed God to call me back into those structures, back into that institution in order to be a change-agent as the entire church as we know it, is renewed, transformed and re-commissioned to fulfill the Kingdom purposes of God.

God made it clear to me that I can be a part of the institution we call 'church' and still faithfully pour my life into the real church – which is God's called-out people. In fact, the Lord made it very clear that it's simply not possible to change a system from the outside. Just as Jesus Himself could not redeem and re-create humanity without becoming part of us, so too we cannot reform and re-create the church by standing on the sideline yelling at the players on the field, hoping the outcome of the game will be different. The only way the game will change is by getting back on the field and staying there to show your teammates a better way and the real purpose of them being out there.

If we truly want to stop 'going to church' and start 'being the church' then we need to accept that the majority of what we have experienced as 'church' throughout our lives is man-made and part of an organization, an institution we have built and it did not necessarily come from God and it certainly didn't come from the New Testament! But somewhere, beneath all the structures, programs, regulations, activities and buildings is the church which Jesus promised to build and the church God has called me to devote my life to finding and re-connecting God's people to its heart, which is the mission of Christ. To do that we need to get back the New Testament – and once again *'... devote ourselves to the Apostles teaching, to fellowship to the breaking of bread and to prayer ..'* (Acts 2:42) as we re-capture the vision and the purpose of the church Jesus birthed and promised to build.

What is the purpose of that church? Why are we all still here? We are here to advance the Kingdom of God, by His grace and for His glory. What is the Kingdom of God? It is the rule and reign of Jesus Christ - as it has always been in heaven, so shall it increasingly be on earth. The church does not have a mission – Jesus Christ has a mission and that mission has a church. The mission of Christ is the only mission the church has ever had. That's why Jesus commissioned us to go and make disciples and teach them everything He has taught us. What did Jesus teach about more than anything else? The Kingdom of God. Then He told His disciples to pray, believing that this Kingdom of God would increasingly manifest on earth: *"Your kingdom come, Your will be done on earth as it is in heaven ..."*

It's all about the Kingdom of God breaking into the kingdom of this world. It has never been about 'converts' or 'members' of an organization. Our primary mission is not to maintain or grow an organization and call it church. We are not called to recruit volunteers to a worthy cause. We are not called to be the social conscience of society. We are not called to be a refugee advocacy group, an environmental watchdog or campaigners for social action, justice and equality. As wonderful as those pursuits may be, none of them are the mission of Christ and yet that is where a growing number of Christians spend most of their time in the name of the church. The mission of Christ is to make disciples and teach them everything Jesus has taught us.

What is a disciple? A disciple is someone who has met Jesus, has been overwhelmed by His love and grace, has fallen in love with Him, embraced His free gift of salvation and His mission, and dedicated themselves to its fulfilment in and through their own lives and their own circle of influence. How is that possible? By His grace, which He has lavished upon us in the life, death, resurrection and empowering presence of Jesus Christ through His Holy Spirit. To what end do we do all this? The glory of God. The more we help Jesus usher in His kingdom right here and now, the more God is lifted up and glorified. The more God is glorified, the more He empowers the mission of Christ to reconcile His lost children to their heavenly Father.

So where do all those other noble causes fit into this purpose of the church? Will we not still care about the marginalized and oppressed? Will we not be concerned about our environment and about justice for all people? Of course we will – but none of that is the primary purpose of the church. The mission of Christ is to the advance the kingdom of God by introducing people to Jesus and making them His disciples. All manner of fruit will <u>then</u> flow out of the fulfilment of that mission – more fruit than we could ever imagine. All those social concerns and issues will be impacted as the <u>fruit of the Gospel</u> impacts our world around us. But the fruit is not the tree! Social action and advocacy must flow out of the gospel and the life of Christ in our midst - they should never replace the gospel. If they do, we are no longer part of the church which Jesus is building – we are part of something else – noble and worthy perhaps – but it's not the church.

We must get back to the core purpose of the church which is to partner with Jesus in the fulfilment of <u>His</u> mission. We need to get back to the place where it's all about Jesus; all about His Kingdom rule and reign; all about the gospel, the good news of Who Jesus is and what He has done and promised to do; where it's all about bringing the power and reality of heaven to earth which is what Jesus did when He was here and what He has commissioned us to continue doing.

That is why I talk a lot about the presence of God, in Christ, through the Holy Spirit. That is why I am always pointing people away from me, away from the institution of the church and towards God, Who is present and alive and real and active in our midst every day. What does all that look like? Well, strap yourselves in because that is the ride we will be taking together in this book as we discover afresh, or perhaps for the first time, what being the church really means. May God continue to open our minds and our hearts and give us a fresh vision of the church.

CHAPTER FIVE
The Church is the Hope of the World

When it's functioning properly, the church of Jesus Christ is the hope of the world. It's the only force on this whole planet, which is capable of healing broken lives, pointing people to God and fulfilling the deepest longings of our souls. It's in the church that the rejected find acceptance, sinners receive forgiveness and the lonely experience love. It's in the church that we discover and encounter God and live out our true life-purpose. *This is worship.*

It's in the church that we receive mentoring, teaching, and training for how we can be the people that God has called us to be as we embrace the mission of Christ. *This is discipleship.* When the church of Jesus Christ is functioning properly, each member is using his or her God-given gifts, talents and abilities to serve one another and the world around them. *This is ministry.*

There's also a very rich, supernatural sense of community within the church of Jesus Christ, that fulfils our longing for friendship and intimacy with others. *This is fellowship.* When the church is functioning properly, the lost - those who are yet to embrace the gospel of Jesus Christ - receive the opportunity to embrace Christ as their Saviour and come within the folds of the church and experience everything mentioned above. *This is evangelism.*

Let me say it again: when it's functioning properly, the church which Jesus Christ birthed and promised to build, truly is the hope of the world. So, over the next few chapters I am going to spend some time looking at the type of church that God wants us to be – not the kind of church we 'attend' or 'align ourselves with' but the kind of church we truly <u>are</u> in our essence. It's not enough that we go to a building on Sundays; it's not enough that we sing songs, take communion, give our tithes and offerings, sit through the sermon; it's not enough that we come to a gathering we call the church if we fail to truly <u>be</u> the church.

So, as we continue this study, we will be looking at closing verses of Acts chapter 2 in order to examine the characteristics of the church which Jesus birthed and promised to build. The Spirit had come upon Peter and the other apostles and they preached the gospel of Christ in Jerusalem with great success. A large number of people believed the gospel that was preached and embraced the salvation offered in Christ. Hence, the church was born. Let's see once again what that looked like:

> *Those who accepted his message were baptized, and about three thousand were added to their number that day. They devoted themselves to the apostles' teaching and to the fellowship, to the breaking of bread and to prayer. Everyone was filled with awe, and many wonders and miraculous signs were done by the apostles.*
>
> *All the believers were together and had everything in common. Selling their possessions and goods, they gave to anyone as he had need. Every day they continued to meet together in the temple courts. They broke bread in their homes and ate together with glad and sincere hearts, praising God and enjoying the favour of all the people. And the Lord added to their number daily those who were being saved. (Acts 2:41–47)*

This church had five important characteristics which I want to focus on now. Let me give you an overview in five clear points.

1. *The church grows warmer through fellowship*

That's what the church we read about was doing.

> *They devoted themselves to the apostles' teaching and to the fellowship. (v.42)*
>
> *All the believers were together and had everything in common. Selling their possessions and goods, they gave to anyone as he had need. Every day they continued to meet together in the temple courts. They broke bread in their homes and ate together with glad and sincere hearts. (vv. 44-46)*

They were devoted to fellowship. They were sharing their lives with each other. They were becoming a family. We live in a world where families are fragmenting and disintegrating. We know that divorce is an ever-present reality. But it's not just divorce that causes families to splinter. We live in a mobile society. Kids grow up and move away. People move in and move out of neighbourhoods and homes because of job transfers and new opportunities. While some people have lived in the same place for most of their lives, there are many other people today who did not grow up the area they now call home. Many of their extended family live far away, and they may find ourselves somewhat displaced and lonely.

We live in a world where 'family' is no longer a constant for many people; no longer something we can count on. All around us there are people who feel disconnected, who long for a closeness with other people, but they don't know where to find it. They try the bowling club, the golf club and various other community groups but something is still missing. Do you remember watching *The Waltons* on television many years ago? Do you remember how everyone lived together - grandma, grandpa: Zeb and Esther Walton; mum and dad: John and Olivia Walton; and seven children: John-Boy, Jason, Mary-Ellen, Erin, Benjamin, Jim-Bob and little Elizabeth. This was a true family and we got to see them in action each week from 1971-1981.

That show tapped into a need in every single one of us. Every member of that family was able to rely upon every other member of the family. Why was that? It was because they were a true family and many of us wish our families were a little more like the Waltons. We long for a simpler time when families stuck together and took care of one another. Some of us may have families like that, but many don't today.

That's why when God created the church, He created it to be a family where real fellowship and community is experienced, where the members can count on one another for support, love and encouragement. That's why God wants us to be a church that grows warmer through fellowship. So, I am hoping we will take some steps in the days ahead to build true fellowship in the church and to make sure that we are functioning the way God wants the church to function. I encourage you to embrace those opportunities as the Holy Spirit leads you deeper into the heart of God and His purpose for His family as the church grows warmer through fellowship.

2. *The church grows deeper through discipleship*

'Discipleship' is a word that basically means, 'learning to follow Jesus.' That is what the church that we read about in Acts 2 was doing. *"They devoted themselves to the apostles' teaching." (v.42)*

These Christians wanted to grow in their new relationship with God in Christ and mature in their Christian walk. They wanted to learn about Jesus so they could become like Jesus. So, they were devoted to what those who had been with Jesus were teaching them. Devoted is a word that means 'committed to' or 'dedicated to.' These first Christians were committed to learning what it means to follow Jesus. God wants the church to be like that. He wants the church to be filled with men, women and young people who genuinely want to follow Jesus and embrace His mission more each day. God wants people who are excited to learn about Jesus and grow in their understanding of His mission and His purpose for us, in us and through us.

Is that you? Are you still excited to learn about Jesus after all these years? How committed are you to sit at His feet and hang off His every word? How devoted are you to the Apostles teaching, which for us is the New Testament? It is my prayer that we will all re-commit to being the type of church that really seeks to learn how to follow Jesus so we might grow deeper through discipleship.

3. *The church grows stronger through worship*

That's what the church in Acts 2 was doing. Verse 42 talks about how they were devoting themselves to *"the breaking of bread"* which partly refers to celebrating Communion together, *"and to prayer."* And then verse 47 says they were *"praising God."* These words are worship language. These people were taking time out to worship God. God has created us with the desire to worship Him and when we fail to worship God, something is missing in our lives; we lose our perspective when God is not placed above everything else we experience. When we lose that perspective, worldly pleasures and worldly values take over. That's why we are surrounded by people in our world who have money, health and fancy lifestyles, but are still searching for something to fill an emptiness inside them which will only ever be filled by them reaching out to the God Who is reaching out to them. There is a God-shaped vacuum inside every human being which longs to be filled.

Have you ever noticed how great you feel when you have truly worshiped God? Worship is something we give to God – it's us praising God for Who He is and for all His goodness to us. But worship is also something that ministers to us; worship is something that reminds us Who God is and boosts our faith and trust in Him to get us through another day and use us in some way to further His Kingdom.

4. *The church grows broader through ministry*

Some think that the reason congregations appoints a Pastor is so he/she can 'do the work of the church.' I hope you don't have that misconception. The truth is, every member is a 'minister of the gospel' in the church. God has given every Christian gifts to use for Him. The only way the church can function as it should is if every disciple of Jesus is using those gifts to advance the Kingdom of God and build up the Body of Christ. That's what the people were doing in Acts 2. The Apostles certainly played a role in leading the way and good leadership is very important. However, all the people were letting God use each of them to minister to each other and that's how they created such a strong community of faith.

That's really what ministry in the church entails: using the gifts God has given us to meet the needs of others and to be a blessing to God as we advance His Kingdom on earth. Now a problem we can see in many church communities is that 'ministry' and 'service' have been defined too narrowly.

Teaching Sunday School is defined as service; leading singing is service; serving communion is service; but if you can't do one of these 'up-front' things, in many churches you feel like you must not have any gifts to use to serve. However, the Bible says that <u>every</u> Christian has been given gifts, talents and abilities by God to use for Him and the Bible lists a wide range of such gifts, talents and abilities beyond those highlighted in most churches.

What we need to understand is that the Bible's lists of gifts are not exhaustive – these are just examples of the many gifts God bestows on the church and the church is only truly functioning as God desires when every member is using their gifts to glorify God.

Part of my job as a Pastor and leader has been to help people discover the gifts God has given the church through them. Each person's job as a disciple of Christ is to put their gifts into action, thereby helping the church become all that God wants it to be. That is how the church grows broader through ministry.

5. *The church grows larger through evangelism*

When the people of God are devoting themselves to the Apostles teaching and making that sincere commitment to fellowship, discipleship, ministry and worship, there is a natural outflow from that and we call it evangelism. This is just a big word which means reaching people with the gospel of Christ and having them respond.

I have always believed that evangelism is not something we do. It's not a task as much as it is an outcome. True evangelism is the fruit of everything else we do. True evangelism is the natural outflow of a healthy church. Acts 2:47 shows us this truth more clearly than any other verse in the New Testament. After giving us a clear overview of what the early Christians were doing day by day, we are then told the fruit of that ministry:

And the Lord added to their number daily those who were being saved. (v.47)

Acts 2 does not provide a magic bullet or a failsafe formula for being the church, but it does provide us with a very clear picture of what was important to our brothers and sisters all those years ago when this wonderful community we call the church was born. We also know from church history that this new church continued to grow at a phenomenal rate and impacted the world around it in immeasurable ways for over two hundred years! That's as long as the modern nation of Australia has existed. Can you even imagine what this nation would be like if the Christian church in Australia continued grow at the rate the early church grew – for 200 hundred years? Can you imagine what our society would be like today? Well, that's what Jesus intended from the beginning! That's why we are all still here.

We don't need some new church growth technique; we don't need a different way to be the church in the 21st century – we just need to go back to our roots and discover how people just like us managed to get it so right for so long! Whatever they were doing and not doing, however they were living out their faith, it was worked – and for a very, very long time! We really need to know why it worked and why it stopped working. Discoveries like that will give us the key to truly being the church as Jesus intended.

There are undoubtedly some cultural realities in the early church which simply do not exist in our nation today. However, the true message of Acts chapter 2 has nothing at all to do with culture. It is a timeless message, a life-changing, church-defining, nation-transforming message and I am really looking forward to re-discovering that reality as we continue this study together.

CHAPTER SIX
Worship God

In the last book of the Bible, the Apostle John shares with us a series of visions he was given – a revelation from God. He saw into heaven's throne room and witnessed the glory of God seated on a throne. He saw Jesus, appearing at times as a Lamb slain for God's people and at other times as a great Conqueror, waging war and riding upon a white horse followed by the armies of heaven. He saw strange images of beasts and dragons, bowls and trumpets, all signifying and symbolizing the colossal struggle taking place between the forces of God and the forces of Satan.

John saw the end of earth's history – the time when Satan is defeated and vanquished for all time, and he witnessed the new heavens and new earth where God's people live in happiness forever. When John was shown this final scene of God's ultimate triumph and the joy of God's people, he was so overwhelmed with emotion that he fell down to worship the angel who had been showing him all these things. Here is the angel's response:

> *Don't do that! I am a fellow servant with you ... Worship God! (Revelation 22:9)*

If we were to summarize the teaching of the Bible in just a few sentences, one of them would have to be this two-word sentence spoken by the angel to John: *Worship God!* The Bible presents God as the One Who is worthy of worship, and repeatedly calls us to give Him our worship and place Him at the centre of everything. In the previous chapter we explored the five characteristics of the New Testament church which God wants to see in every church community: worship, discipleship, fellowship, ministry, and evangelism. In this chapter we will explore the first of those: worship.

In chapter 4 of John's gospel we read where Jesus was talking with the woman from Samaria, and she asked Jesus to settle an argument about where people should worship. Instead, Jesus talked about the type of worship that pleases God.

> *"Sir," the woman said, "I can see that you are a prophet. Our fathers worshiped on this mountain, but you Jews claim that the place where we must worship is in Jerusalem." Jesus declared, "Believe me, woman, a time is coming when you will worship the Father neither on this mountain nor in Jerusalem. You Samaritans worship what you do not know; we worship what we do know, for salvation is from the Jews. Yet a time is coming and has now come when the true worshipers will worship the Father in spirit and truth, for they are the kind of worshipers the Father seeks. God is spirit, and his worshipers must worship in spirit and in truth." (John 4:19-24)*

Let me remind you of some truths about worship. First of all, we must notice that Jesus says that it is not just 'a God' that we are worshiping - it's our heavenly Father. 'Father' was the preferred name that Jesus used when talking about God. For instance, in the Sermon on the Mount He said things such as, *"Let your light shine before men, that they may see your good deeds and praise your Father in heaven"* (Matthew 5:16) and he told us that *"your Father knows what you need before you ask him."* (Matthew 6:8). He also promised that *"your Father in heaven will give good gifts to those who ask him."* (Matthew 7:11). He taught us to pray by saying, *"Our Father who art in heaven."* (Matthew 6:9) and promised that, *"your heavenly Father will also forgive you."* (Matthew 6:14). There are many other examples, but these suffice to show that Jesus tended to call God 'Father' when He was speaking about Him.

Here, when speaking with this Samaritan woman, Jesus used this 'father' language to talk about God. *"A time is coming when you will worship THE FATHER neither on this mountain nor in Jerusalem ... the true worshipers will worship THE FATHER in spirit and truth, for they are the kind of worshipers THE FATHER seeks."*

Now, at first glance this may not seem like such a big deal, especially to those of us who have been in the church for a while, because we've grown so accustomed to hearing it. However, calling God 'Father' in the time of Jesus was a really big deal. It was actually scandalous because it implied a closeness and a familiarity with God that the teachers of the law said was way beyond our ability to experience. The Pharisees and scribes taught that we are temporal, but God is eternal. We are weak, but God is all-powerful. We are limited, but God has no limits. So, the very idea that we could have a close relationship with God as our 'Father' was totally outrageous to them and yet here was Jesus teaching us to call God out 'Father.' There is a lot of meaning packed into that word.

God is more to us than some all-powerful distant being; He is more than an eternal spirit; He is more than an all-knowing entity; He is more than the creator and king of the universe. If that was all we could say God was, there would still be plenty of reason to worship Him. He would still deserve our worship and we would still have reason to give it. But God is far more than that! Not only is He an all-powerful God Who created us, He is our Father Who loves us and cares for us. Not only is He an all-knowing entity Who knows us totally, everything about us, even our thoughts, He is our Father Who loves us anyway, in spite of what He knows about us. Not only is He the king of the universe, He is our Father Who protects us, provides for us and fixes things when they break.

Therefore, the reality of who God is, changes our motivation for worship. It's not just that we worship a king because He requires us to, we worship our Father Who loves us and cares for us. It's not just that we worship an all-powerful being who could force us to if He wanted to, we freely worship our Father Who loves us and protects us. It's not just a god we are worshiping – it is our Father, with all that word entails. When we reflect on that - on Who it is we are worshiping - it changes our view of worship from an activity that we think we have to do because God desires it, to something we get to do because God loves us, and we want to thank Him and honour Him and praise Him.

This leads us to another truth about worship: It's not the 'dressings' of worship that are important; it's the heart of the worshiper that really matters. The woman in our passage above mentions a debate between the Jews and the Samaritans which had been going on for hundreds of years. That debate centred around the question of where the proper place was to worship God. The Jews said that the proper place for worship was the Temple in Jerusalem, while the Samaritans taught that God wanted to be worshiped on top of Mount Gerizim, a mountain of Samaria. They were both hung up on what we might call the 'dressings' of worship - the external, outward signs of worship that we tend to think must be present in order for worship to occur. For us that might be things like church buildings and singing songs and preaching sermons and all those other up-front things we value. These things may be good, but they aren't what makes worship, *true* worship. In fact, you can have all these things and still not actually worship God. Conversely, you can have none of those things and still have true worship.

The Jews and Samaritans were hung up on the externals of worship and Jesus said they were both wrong. He said, *"a time is coming when you will worship the Father neither on this mountain nor in Jerusalem."* Jesus was right. Within just a short period of time, Roman armies would put an end to the formal worship of God in both of those places. Jesus said that true worshipers would worship the Father *"in spirit and in truth."* This phrase means *"worshiping God in sincerity and honesty, led by the Spirit of God."* It is when we humbly come before God, drawn by His Spirit, and offer Him our praise and adoration for Who He is and all He has done, recognising our dependence upon Him for our salvation, our life and for everything! It is the Holy Spirit Who draws us into this place of transparency and honesty before God.

We cannot worship God in spirit until our spirit has been overwhelmed or captured by His Spirit. That is the place true worship comes from within us. God is not really interested in lip-service worship, even if it happens in a church building and is offered in the name of Jesus. He doesn't want us to sing songs or pray prayers while our hearts are somewhere else. He doesn't want us to take communion when our thoughts aren't centred on Jesus and the power and reality of His atoning death. God isn't interested in us sitting politely while a preacher shares God's Word, when our mind is not engaged at all.

By the same token, this means that you can worship God, even when you are not in a church building. It means that you can worship God, even if your singing voice isn't all that great. It means that you can worship God, whether you are with other people or by yourself. Because our worship is not confined to a place, we can and we should worship God every day. We can worship God anytime we pause to reflect on how wonderful He is and offer Him our praise. Every time we sing a song praising God and really mean it - whether in a church building or in the shower or in the car - we are worshiping. Every time we thank God for how amazing He is to us, we are worshiping. Every time we read the Scriptures and draw near to God with hearts open to hear what the Holy Spirit is saying, we are worshiping God because we are saying to Him that He is important enough to draw near to, to listen to, to seek wisdom from and to follow every day of our lives.

Worship is not a Sunday activity only, any more than it was a Jerusalem Temple or Mount Gerizim activity only. Worship is about honouring God with our lives by praising Him for how good and wonderful He is. Worship should take place every day, because God is worthy of our worship every day! When we save worship for Sunday; when we make worship something that can only occur within the walls of a particular building - we are falling into the same trap which snared the Samaritans and the Jews. And Jesus says, *"Don't be like that! God is calling you to worship Him in spirit and in truth."*

How timely is this reminder given what we experienced recently with the global pandemic? We were all forced into exile from our 'temples' and meeting places. Like those Jews and Samaritans, we needed to also learn that God does not dwell in buildings made by man, regardless of how consecrated they may be. God is not tied to an event, a meeting, or a worship 'service' at a designated time and place. God is ever-present and will receive our worship regardless of our location or what day of the week it might be. Worship comes from a sincere heart, full of praise and thanksgiving as we acknowledge God's greatness, majesty, grace, love, mercy and His central place in our lives.

So, when we see the early church in action in Acts chapter 2, we see a people who worshiped God every day; a people who placed God and His mission at the very centre of everything. Herein lies the most important reality concerning worship and if you remember nothing else from this chapter, remember this: to truly worship God, we must place Him at the centre of everything, 24 hours a day, 7 days a week.

In John chapter 5 we read where Jesus said that He only did what He saw the Father doing (v.19) and only spoke the words the Father gave Him to speak (v.30). What does that mean? Quite simply it means that Jesus intentionally placed the Father at the centre of His life – everything was about His will, His glory, His purpose, His plan, His desires and His Kingdom. When Jesus did that, He modelled true worship for us. True worship, at its best, is when only doing what you see God doing, only speaking the words God gives you to speak becomes your daily priority, your goal, your purpose and your very life.

Then, and only then, will you understand and experience the fullness of worship. Then you will be able to wake up every morning and immediately think of God first. You will thank Him for gifting you another new day. Then you will immediately start asking two questions and you won't stop asking them until your head hits the pillow that night. *"What are You doing, Lord?"* and *"How can I be part of it?"* When you open the Scriptures for your quiet time; when you switch on the news or read the morning paper; when you go for your morning walk around your local neighbourhood: *"What are You doing, Lord? … How can I be part of it?"* When you join with your brothers and sisters for worship, you will know that the only thing on your mind and in your heart will be discovering what God is doing in the midst of His gathered people; what He is saying to His disciples and how you can respond.

When that is all that matters, then this is worship. I don't care if you think the sermons are too long or too short; the music is too old or new, too fast or slow. None of that matters to God. The only thing that matters is your attitude and your desire to truly encounter God – to see what He is doing and hear what He is saying and be an active part of Christ's mission on earth. For Jesus to say that He only did what He saw the Father doing and only spoke the words the Father gave Him to speak – it meant that His entire demeanour every moment of every day He was among us, was one of looking to and listening for the Father.

It doesn't take a high IQ to work out that if you are not looking intentionally for something, you will most probably not find it and if you are not listening intentionally for someone you will most probably miss what they're saying! Yet I suggest there are millions of people across the world right now who claim to be disciples of Jesus, but they fail to understand this most basic, defining reality of Jesus' entire life and ministry. Every step Jesus took; every miracle He performed; every sermon He preached; every prayer He prayed; every decision He made; were all in response to what He first observed His Father doing and saying.

This is worship! This is the Christian life! This is the most important lesson Jesus taught us. This is why He remained among us for three years as a man – so He could role-model how we are meant to live and worship.

> *Therefore, I urge you, brothers and sisters, in view of God's mercy, to offer your bodies as a living sacrifice, holy and pleasing to God – this is your true and proper worship. Do not conform to the pattern of this world, but be transformed by the renewing of your mind. Then you will be able to test and approve what God's will is – his good, pleasing and perfect will. (Romans 12:1-2)*

When Paul says we are to present our bodies as a living sacrifice and that this is true worship, he is not talking about our physical bodies – he is talking about our entire being. He is talking about us being totally surrendered and then totally transformed so that God is at the centre of everything. This is true worship. This is true Christianity.

This is how the kingdom of heaven will be advanced on this earth as God's will unfolds before our eyes. All that begins when you open your eyes in the morning and the first thing that comes to mind is, *"What are you doing Lord? How can I be part of it?"*

You may not have an answer immediately - when we are so out of practice, it takes time to recognize the hand of God at work; it takes time to discern His voice above our own and all the other voices which seek to dominate His. But in time, you will see; in time, you will hear and you will become part of the mission of Christ to bring every man, woman and young person into the glory of the Kingdom of God.

Then you will know what true worship is. Then, you will know why God allows us to continue living in this broken and needy world. Then, you will know the first and most important component of truly being the church.

CHAPTER SEVEN
In His Steps

In the late 1800's a book was published by Charles Sheldon called *In His Steps*. The story begins with a preacher, hard at work on a sermon. His text is 1 Peter 2:21: *"...Christ suffered for you, leaving you an example, that you should follow in his steps."* The rest of the book then offers what is a very honest and powerful explanation of what following in Jesus' steps actually looks like. As we have been exploring what being the church really means, we have been examining the traits that God wants to be present in the church which Jesus promised to build. In the last chapter we talked about how God wants us to be a church that worships and we discussed what true worship entails. In this chapter we will see that God wants us to be a church that learns from Jesus so that we can continue His mission on earth. In other words – we need to be a church of disciples.

> *The student is not above the teacher, but everyone who is fully trained will be like their teacher. (Luke 6:40)*

The context in which Jesus said this makes it plain that He considered this the goal for His followers: to follow in His steps. That is Jesus' expectation of us: everyone who is fully trained will be like his/her teacher. I am sure this is what Jesus had in mind when he uttered these words:

> *Come to me, all you who are weary and burdened, and I will give you rest. Take my yoke upon you and learn from me, for I am gentle and humble in heart, and you will find rest for your souls. For my yoke is easy and my burden is light. (Matthew 11:28-30)*

The expression, *"Take My yoke upon you"* actually meant *"Become my disciple,"* or *"Become my follower and walk in my steps."* Our world says that you can't live that way. It's just not possible. Some in the church even believe we cannot live that way – Jesus was the Son of God, only He could live that way.

Now, at this point, I could tell you the world is wrong; that you should do what Jesus did because His way is right and you will be a better spouse, a better parent, a better child, a better employee, a better person and that Jesus called us to live this way; I could also talk about how a life lived in devotion to God and His teaching is fun and exciting and fulfilling; I could even argue today that the very best life you can have is one that is lived fully and completely for God's glory. But notice that Jesus doesn't make any of those arguments or discuss any of those things. He just says that if we take His yoke upon ourselves, learn from Him and walk in His steps, *He will give us rest.*

This word *rest* is actually a promise of heaven. If we become His disciples, He will give us heaven - rest from the problems of this life; rest from its pain; rest from sickness and sorrow, disease and death. He will give us Heaven. Now hopefully we know by now that when Jesus talks about heaven He is not only talking about our future hope after death. He is also talking about the here-and-now. Heaven on earth. Jesus is promising that if we will become His disciples and learn from Him and walk in His steps and fulfill His mission, we will increasingly experience this *rest* of heaven right now – the *rest* from life's weariness, the *rest* from life's burdens. In other words, He will answer our prayer, *"Your kingdom come, your will be done on earth as it is in heaven."*

Let's face it: Life at times is hard. It seems like sometimes you are doing fine, and then the storm hits, the wind screams, the dam bursts, the raging torrents flood us. Sometimes it's marriage problems; or children problems; or parent problems; or work problems; or health problems; or church problems. All sorts of challenges, difficulties and struggles make up this experience we call life. Life can often make us weary to the point of despair as we carry burdens that would crush the best of us. So, into that cold, hard reality Jesus speaks:

"Come to me, all you who are weary and burdened, and I will give you rest. Take my yoke upon you and learn from me, for I am gentle and humble in heart, and you will find rest for your souls." (Matthew 11:28-29)

Jesus promises us rest from our burdens if we'll be His disciples, because He is gentle and humble, and He gives us a kind of rest deep in our souls which the world can never give; our loved ones can never give; only Jesus can give us this rest.

That doesn't mean Jesus frees His followers from ever having problems in this life. When Jesus promised rest, He did not mean that He would remove our problems, but rather that He will give us the strength to make it through our problems. He will give us the comfort and peace we need to face any challenge, any tragedy; He will help us experience real joy in this life because we know Him. But He will not give us this strength overnight or by a magical touch. Such strength comes through learning and growing in Christ, day by day, month by month, year by year. It comes by walking in His steps.

Jesus promises that if we will take His yoke upon ourselves and learn from Him, every day, every week, for all our lives – then and only then will we truly find rest in Him, in spite of our circumstances. Then and only then will we walk in His steps. He will give us a taste of heaven here and now and sustain us in the face of life's burdens and weariness. When we begin to learn from Jesus; when we begin to learn the words that He spoke and the things that He taught and did, we discover all these treasures that we didn't even know existed before. We find a peace we never dreamed of; we experience a hope brighter than any other and we receive guidance to help us figure life out. As we learn Christ's words and apply them in our lives, we discover what the Apostle Paul really meant when he said:

> *I have been crucified with Christ and I no longer live, but Christ lives in me. (Galatians 2:20)*

The whole reason Jesus remained among us for three years and taught His disciples all that time, is so they could pass that on to others. When it was time to go, Jesus then commissioned those men and women to go into the world and teach everyone what He had taught them, always knowing that He would be with them at all times through His Holy Spirit.

This is what birthed the church. This is why in that snapshot of the early church in Acts 2:42-47 it tells us that the believers *"devoted themselves to the Apostles teaching."* What was the Apostles teaching then? It was all that Jesus had taught them! What is the Apostles teaching today? To what should we be devoting ourselves now? For all intents and purposes, it is the New Testament. It's really that simple!

This doesn't mean we ignore the Old Testament. It is vitally important in connecting the Christian church and our journey this side of the cross of Christ with the whole Jewish story and their journey as God's people down through history. The entire Bible is important - but the teaching of Jesus, which then became the teaching of the Apostles, which then became the New Testament – is what defines the very nature and purpose of the church. It is what explains the New Covenant in Christ and the whole reason we are still here today. So, it is this teaching that we should be devoting ourselves to and in so doing, we are sitting at the feet of Jesus as His followers, His disciples, His co-labourers in the ministry of the Kingdom of God and the gospel of God's amazing grace!

I think we need to notice the language in Acts 2:42. It says, *"They devoted themselves to the apostles' teaching..."* Luke uses the intense Greek word *proskartereo*, often translated as "*devoted to,*" to report on the strength of their commitment here. The word literally means "*to occupy oneself diligently with something*" or "*to persist in.*" So, if being the church is important to us, we will be occupying ourselves diligently with the Apostles teaching. We will be persistent in our devotion to hearing God's voice through the teaching of His anointed, called leaders and teachers.

Now I'm not sure what you think about preaching, teaching and authority and how God speaks to His people today. I am not sure where you place people like me who devote their lives to being oracles of God and conduits of His life-changing Word. But you need to wrestle with this question if being the church is important to you in any way. Even a cursory reading of the Bible will show us that God speaks to His people in a myriad of ways. He speaks through creation. He will speak through a talking donkey if He needs to! He will also use any human being to bear witness to His Word. However, the most common way God has spoken to His people is through a messenger - through prophets and teachers whom He calls, equips and sends across the earth with His message. I have such a calling on my life, and I take that calling very seriously in my preaching, teaching, writing and all aspects of ministry.

I have also been doing this long enough to know that God can and does deliver His Word, His will and His empowering through this crazy thing the Apostle Paul called *'the foolishness of preaching.'* He called it foolishness because most days, from our end, that is exactly how it feels. How on earth can I even dream of being the channel of God's voice to others? How can a fallen, sinful, imperfect person be used by God to speak life, hope and power into other human beings? Foolishness indeed! However, it only seems like foolishness if we lose sight of this being the primary means God uses to communicate to His people.

The Scriptures we value so highly and upon which our faith is based, are nothing but a collection of the stories, teaching and preaching of fallible people like me whom God has raised up to speak His truth, write His truth and declare His Word at every point in history. Yet for that teaching to actually impact our hearts and lives or change the way we live and relate to each other and to God, we need to embrace it. We need to respect it. We need to believe it is God Who still chooses to speak this way. We need *proskartereo* – <u>devotion</u> to this teaching. I hope and pray that the fact you are even reading this book, is an indication of your devotion to God's Word and will.

It doesn't matter how passionate or gifted the teacher is; it doesn't matter if the teacher is Jesus or the Apostles or preachers and teachers today. Those who are being taught must decide if they will devote themselves to that teaching and embrace it. If they don't, then the Word of God will continue to elude them and the power of His Kingdom will remain a future hope, not a present reality. As a preacher, I know of no greater joy than to see someone devoting themselves to this teaching and to then respond to God's Word through something I have said or written and to see their life totally transformed by His Word. I still have letters and cards from people over the past thirty years who have shared how their entire lives were turned upside down and inside out because of teaching they received from God, through me. How is that possible? It's not because I'm a great preacher. It happened because those people knew and understood what 'devoting themselves to the Apostles teaching' really meant. They took responsibility for their own spiritual life and growth. They persisted in digesting every morsel of truth from every sermon, blog or book. This is what 'devoting themselves to' actually looks like.

When we truly devote ourselves to the Apostles teaching, we truly become disciples of Jesus and everything in our life will change - and I mean everything! I know this from my personal experience and the experience of hundreds of men, women and young people whom I have seen totally transformed before my eyes. People whose lives are never the same again and all they did was make a daily choice to deliberately, intentionally and persistently engage with the teaching in their local church. That's all they did. God did the rest.

Sadly, most of the words preached by God's messengers across this nation hit the floor dead before any of them have a chance to lodge in someone's heart. How do I know that? I know that because the church is not in revival and this nation is not on its knees before God! I know that because our congregations are shrinking; our sermons are getting shorter; too much of our preaching is no longer Christ-centred and fewer and fewer people are really listening for God in the sermons they hear.

Jesus commissioned us to go and make disciples. He didn't tell us to go and make converts for our religious club. He said make disciples – <u>His</u> disciples! And we see what a disciple is in Acts chapter 2. They are the ones who devoted themselves to the Apostles' teaching, which was the teaching of Jesus. They chose to take His yoke upon them and learn from Him. They were devoted to this important learning process – not just at the beginning – but for their entire life! That's what a disciple does and that's what being the church has to be all about or we are not the church that Jesus is building! We are nothing but a hollow religion with a dusty ancient book and some powerless rhetoric passed on from a dead, powerless teacher. In Jesus' name I implore you, listen to what the Spirit of God is saying to the church today.

God will not continue sending His servants to preach His Word to people who are not listening. God is patient. God is gracious. But God is also firmly committed to the mission of Jesus Christ to advance His Kingdom on earth and He will not waste His Word or His servants on people who don't want to change; don't want to grow; don't want to live and move and have their being in Christ as His disciples. Jesus doesn't need friends. Jesus doesn't need PR people. Jesus doesn't need lip-service. Jesus doesn't need our latest programs or our great innovations or our trendy ministry ideas. Jesus needs disciples. That's the only thing He has ever needed. That was His entire purpose in coming to earth. His birth, life, ministry, death and resurrection all pointed to one objective – making disciples who could join Him in fulfilling His mission to reconcile all of God's lost children to their heavenly Father.

Sadly, the church of today seems to have many priorities. Our focus has been drawn towards all manner of good deeds and community programs and welfare initiatives and ministries which bless people. However, Jesus birthed a church which had a singular focus and it never, ever strayed from that intentional focus. Jesus called and commissioned us to do exactly what He was called and commissioned to do: make disciples. But we cannot make disciples until we really learn how to be disciples ourselves. Then, and only then, will we understand what being the church really means.

CHAPTER EIGHT
Our Partnership with God

Even a casual glance at the book of Acts in the Bible will reveal the phenomenal impact the church had on the world in those first few hundred years. All of that changed when believers were lured into a new paradigm by the Roman Emperor at the time and we adopted the ways of the world and let go of the very things which brought success to the church in those early days. That unbelievable growth rate, together with the unprecedented influence the church had on the world, were sacrificed and we have been paying the price ever since. Our experience of church today is therefore radically different to how it once was.

So why is that such a big deal? The church is still here, and we still have people coming to faith and embracing the gospel of Jesus Christ, albeit not at the same rate that they were in the beginning. Isn't it a good thing the church has not disappeared altogether? Is it really a big deal that we don't have the influence we once had in the world? Excellent questions. I look forward to providing some answers as we continue this study.

Our response will depend on what we think the church is here for and what we think God expects of the church in any age. What is our purpose? Is growing the church an end in itself? Or does God have a much higher and broader expectation for the disciples of Jesus Christ? Well, you may need to brace yourself for what I say next. God's expectations for the church Jesus promised to build are far greater than most of us would ever imagine. In fact, God expects His people to be the means by which He solves <u>all</u> the problems of the world. When you look across the earth today and see the level of dysfunction, moral decay, corruption and evil, I wonder if you realise that God is expecting His people, the church, to fulfil their calling so He can solve all those problems through the church? I would like us to look again at a verse which I believe is one of the most important verses in the Bible for the church of today.

Even though it was written over 2,400 years ago in a radically different setting, it is one of those verses which transcends time, culture and location. That's because it contains a promise from God which has never been withdrawn and is even more relevant today than when these words were first uttered.

> *If my people who are called by my name, will humble themselves and pray, and seek my face and turn from their wicked ways, then I will hear from heaven, forgive their sin, and heal their land.*
> (2 Chronicles 7:14)

I have never seen a time in my life, when there was a greater need for the healing of nations, the healing of cities, the healing of the land. This verse has never been more in our face than it is today. Now, as I am sure you know, there are certain words from the Lord that are so inconvenient that they're easy to ignore, or just bypass. They are so demanding that they are easy to downplay or relegate to a specific group of people other than us. This verse is such a word from God.

Please note that God did <u>not</u> say, "*If the pagan sinners would just stop sinning, I'll heal the land.*" Note also that God did <u>not</u> say, "*If those in authority who are making ungodly decisions and infecting the mindsets of the people, if they would repent, then I'll heal the land.*" God didn't say that. He actually said, "*If my people ... will do what only they can do ... then I will heal their land.*" It almost sounds as if God is suggesting that the fate of the whole world rests in the hands of His people.

Surely God is not saying we are responsible for other people's actions. Someone else's sin is not my sin, so why should I take responsibility for what others have done? I must confess my sin and repent of my bad choices and actions but surely, I cannot be held accountable for what others do.

Well, that kind of thinking and reasoning is so typical of the modern, enlightened mindset and therein lies one of our greatest problems. Let me remind you of someone who didn't think this way. Nehemiah was a righteous man, but he prayed as though the sins of the people were his sins.

> *"Lord, the God of heaven, the great and awesome God, who keeps his covenant of love with those who love him and keep his commandments, let your ear be attentive and your eyes open to hear the prayer your servant is praying before you day and night for your servants, the people of Israel. I confess the sins we Israelites, including myself and my father's family, have committed against you. We have acted very wickedly toward you. We have not obeyed the commands, decrees and laws you gave your servant Moses." (Nehemiah 1:5-7)*

It is so hard for us to understand Nehemiah's actions here. We've grown up in the modern western world where individualism is almost worshipped, and any sense of communal responsibility has long been forgotten. The prevailing view is, *'You do your thing, I do my thing, others do their thing, and I am only responsible for my actions.'* Strictly speaking, that is true. However, in our current individualistic culture we have lost sight of any sense of being 'a people.' Communal or corporate responsibility is a concept rarely mentioned and almost never accepted.

2 Chronicles 7:14 begins, *"If my people, who are called by my name ..."* and when God says those words He is not thinking individually. When He says, *'my people'* He means all of His children. Nehemiah understood this and that is why he took ownership of the sins of others and confessed them before God and cried out for mercy on behalf of all the people who had strayed from God. This gives us such a powerful image of this righteous man confessing the sins of his people as his own. Nehemiah understood that he was part of this community of lost children and so he identified with them personally in this prayer.

Of course, the greatest example we have of a person identifying with all the people whom God loves came many years later when a righteous man Who knew no sin, hung on a cross and became sin – giving his life to atone for the sin of the very people who murdered Him! Jesus so identified with all of humanity, that He even cried out to His heavenly Father with His dying breath as said, *"Father, forgive them for they know not what they do."*

I hear a lot of talk in the church and in sermons about 'them' as opposed to 'us.' We so easily point the finger of blame to those people who are outside the church – the ungodly, unchurched, unenlightened people who are responsible for the state of the world. But if we choose to truly humble ourselves before God and pray and seek His face, something happens deep inside us. There is no 'them' anymore – there is only 'us.'

This is where true intercessory prayer occurs. In the humility of prayer, it doesn't mean that someone else's sin is my sin, but it does mean I so deeply identify in compassion with the people I'm praying for, that I stand among them in prayer, and I say, *"God, forgive us for our sins, for we have sinned against you."* True Spirit-led intercessory prayer means we stand in the shoes of another and plead their case as though it was our own. That is what we so desperately need right now and God is still calling out to us:

> *"If my people, don't wait for somebody else to do it, no politician, no leader, no scientist, no billionaire is going to fix this world, but if my people who are called by my name, will humble themselves and pray, seek my face and turn from their wicked ways, then I will hear from heaven, forgive their sin, and heal their land."*

Something else we seem to have missed with this verse is the magnitude of what God is promising. God doesn't just promise to forgive our sin. God is not just calling us to humble ourselves and pray and confess our sin as a people so we can kiss and make up with our Creator and be on good terms with God again. That, in itself is pretty awesome, but this promise is so much greater than that. God has promised to heal our land when His people do what He has called them to do. But God's intent is far greater than healing the land. He wants the world to know how and why He heals the land. Everything God does is against the backdrop of His mission on earth. His deepest desire is to bring all His lost children home – most of whom don't even believe He exists! He wants to move in power across the land in response to the humility and prayers of His people in such a way that everyone will notice and everyone will know that God is alive, that God's people have His ear and God's power is manifest in our world. God doesn't just want to bless us. God doesn't just want to answer our prayers. God wants His answer and His blessing to be so visible and so amazing that everyone – to the very ends of the earth – will believe and worship their God.

Psalm 67 talks about the people of God coming into a place of blessing and the earth itself then responding and yielding its produce.

> *"May God be gracious to us and bless us and make his face shine on us - so that your ways may be known on earth, your salvation among all nations. May the peoples praise you, God; may all the peoples praise you. May the nations be glad and sing for joy, for you rule the peoples with equity and guide the nations of the earth. May the peoples praise you, God; may all the peoples praise you. The land yields its harvest; God, our God, blesses us. May God bless us still, so that all the ends of the earth will fear him."* (Psalm 67)

I am not sure if you connected with the work of George Otis Jnr. back in the 1990's through his two *'Transformations'* videos, but if you didn't, I would really encourage you to find them on YouTube and watch them - you will be blessed! George has spent most of his life researching mighty moves of God around the world which not only refreshed and revived the church but had a transforming impact on the whole community.

He looked at specific revivals around the world where there were not only huge numbers of people coming to Jesus, but the impact of that expanding, praying, believing church was life-changing for those outside the church – for whole communities and in some cases, entire nations.

One of the most amazing examples of this occurred in a little place in Guatemala by the name of Almolonga. Many are calling it 'the city of miracles' or 'the city of God' because of the radical transformations which took place in almost every aspect of this Mayan community. But just about everything good that can be said about Almolonga is a comparatively recent development.

A number of decades ago their economy was in ruins, the city was plagued with poverty and disease; drug addiction, alcoholism and violence were rampant. Because of these hardships the people of Almolonga had previously sought the help of the ancient Columbian idol, Maximon (pronounced 'Mashimon'). He is a supernatural spirit being that had to be worshiped with offerings of alcohol, tobacco and money. Mayan priests had to be drunk before they could even approach this entity to seek his blessings. As part of the worship ceremony, the priests would give lit cigars or cigarettes to Maximon, and then they'd spit out alcohol on the devotees. It was also the custom in Almolonga to get the children drunk in order to teach them at an early age to be faithful to the idol. The followers of Maximon hoped to get good fortune but what they got instead was an endless cycle of spiritual oppression.

Donato Santiago was the Police Chief of Almolonga for many years. He says there was never any peace. There was a lot of violence towards women. Crowds would gather around the bars every night just to watch the drunks get into fights. Every morning, men who were still drunk or injured from the night before could be found lying in the streets. Santiago needed 12 armed deputies to help him patrol the town. The city had four jails to hold the worst offenders and the jail cells were always full. All this in a small city of less than 20,000 people!

There was a small group of Christians in Almolonga who wanted to change their community but they didn't know how. A Pastor by the name of Mariano Riscajché and a couple of others started having a prayer vigil every night. At first, the spiritual warfare was intense, but after a while, people in the town started getting delivered from the spirit they identified as Maximon. Those being set free from this demonic spirit often coughed up blood or got thrown around the room and some were even flung out into the street.

Among those was a Shaman Priest named José Albino Tazei. He was a respected Priest but he was also a violent alcoholic who was abusive to his wife and children. Without saying anything to him, the prayer group started praying directly for José. After one particular month-long drinking ceremony to honour the idol Maximon, José collapsed against a wall and he could not move a muscle. He cried out to God to save him. Instantly his mind became clear and he was set free from his addictions to alcohol and tobacco. José went home and burned all of his shamanic paraphernalia and the next day he started taking his family to the prayer meetings. This received a lot of community attention.

By now new churches were springing up all over Almolonga but the spiritual battle was not over. The followers of Maximon began to disrupt church services and threatened believers with violence. Evangelists were attacked by vicious mobs and beaten with sticks and shovels. Church windows were smashed with rocks and empty liquor bottles. One night a group of masked men kidnapped pastor Mariano and tried to kill him. Three times they tried to shoot him in the face and three times their guns wouldn't fire. They became so frightened at not being able to kill him that they ran away, leaving Pastor Mariano tied to a chair.

At the same time that this violent opposition was going on, God began to heal many desperately ill people in the city of Almolonga. One of them was a lady named Teresa who actually died after a botched medical procedure but was raised from the dead through prayer. When the news spread that Teresa was alive again, people started flocking to her house to get prayers for healing. As the power of God continued to spread across Almolonga, the Priests of Maximon began to lose all their paying customers. Finally, they packed up their idols and left town!

When they left, the curse that was on Almolonga for so long just seemed to leave with them. Most of the town's 36 bars not closed down, and many of them were converted into storefront churches that began to hold worship services every day of the week. Before this transformation happened in Almolonga, there were three little struggling churches and 36 busy bars. Several months after this amazing transformation there were 33 busy churches and only three little ramshackle bars!

Police Chief Santiago was absolutely amazed at the change. Crime simply disappeared. There was no more unemployment. There was no more violence, no more drunks on the streets.

Almolonga eventually closed down all four jails. One building that once held dangerous criminals was remodelled and began being used for wedding ceremonies. The whole city experienced tremendous economic growth as well. When people started turning to God, the farm fields around Almolonga became so fertile, that they began to yield three huge harvests every year, for the first time in living memory. Before revival broke out, the farmers' cooperative of Almolonga exported approximately four truckloads of produce every month. After God healed their land there were 40 truckloads leaving every week! The carrots being harvested were larger than your arm and the cabbages were the size of basketballs. Some vegetables which once had a sixty-day growing cycle, started to mature in just twenty five days.

Even during droughts in the surrounding areas, the soil in Almolonga was always moist. Underground springs just opened up right across the region to provide a constant source of water for the farms. God literally 'healed the land' as He promised in 2 Chronicles 7:14. These harvests were all so remarkable that agricultural research teams from around the world came to Almolonga to study the soil and their farming methods. Local farmers became rich with many buying up the land in the surrounding communities and hiring people from nearby towns to work the fields. A number of new Mercedes Benz trucks were purchased to ship their produce to market. Pastor Mariano's father, who soon purchased his own farm, was astonished by the progress. He said, *"We never dreamed of selling our produce outside of Guatemala, but now we are exporting to other nations."*

Within a couple of years, almost 90% of the residents of Almolonga called themselves spirit-filled Christians. They even erected a sign at the entrance to the city which read, *'Jesus is Lord of Almolonga.'* By almost any standards, Almolonga became one of the most thoroughly transformed cities in the world and it all started with a small group of God's people who are called by His name, humbling themselves and praying every day. They sought the face of God and identified with the sin of their whole city. God heard their prayers, discerned their hearts, forgave their sin, demolished a demonic stronghold and healed their land.

This was not just a revival of the church, this was the radical and complete transformation of an entire community and that is what God desires to do through us, being the church! There are lots of ways of filling church buildings with people and running a successful organisation in Jesus' name – but God's intent is that through the church, the manifold wisdom of God may be made known (Ephesians 3:10) and that whole cities and entire nations might be completely transformed by the power of God. All of that will happen in response to the humility, repentance, faith and fervent prayers of God's people.

That is our end game; that is where we are headed if we are serious; and that is why we really need to know what it means to be the church. In Christ, we literally hold the key to every problem on this planet. We live and move and have our being in the only One Who can ever redeem God's people and transform whole nations. The degree to which you commit to being the church, will determine what happens not just in your life and your church – but in your whole community and nation – as you touch heaven and change earth every day in so many ways.

The people of Almolonga learned very quickly what being the church really means – and absolutely everything changed around them. There is nothing which will prevent the same city-wide transformation from happening where you live and serve the Lord. I know it is mind-boggling to even contemplate our partnership with God having that kind of impact in our nation, but that is exactly what God intends for His disciples. That is His purpose for the church.

CHAPTER NINE
Koinonia Fellowship

We have been exploring what being the church involves. This requires some study and serious reflection because the church which we've experienced for many generations now is radically different to the church which Jesus birthed so long ago. So, if we truly want to know what being the church means from Jesus' perspective, we have to look beyond the corrupted visible 'church' we have all inherited and known all our lives. You might think the word corrupted is too strong, but I wish I had a much stronger word when I think of how a dynamic, Spirit-led, Christ-centred, relational community could be transformed so radically into what is, more often than not, an event-based, task-centred, rule-governed religion. Or in other cases the church has been reduced to a socio-political welfare agency with little or no reference to Christ or the gospel. You simply cannot look at the early church and the modern church without scratching your head and wondering what happened.

Again, I draw your attention to how it was when the church began. I want you to imagine what it was like; how it worked; where it happened; how it felt; what impact it had on the people who were part of this miracle and the people watching on in the community. You've probably read and heard the closing verses of Acts chapter 2 many times, but please don't let familiarity rob you of the impact of what is actually happening to and through these people; our pioneers; our brothers and sisters in Christ.

As promised by Jesus, the Holy Spirit came on the day of Pentecost and things got very messy, very exciting and very real - and here is the result. Peter got up and told everybody what was really happening and how this was all part of God's plan and how this was exactly what Jesus came to create – a new community of faith – a new covenant of love and grace. Then this new thing we call the church, began to take shape. Let's read those words again:

> *"... They devoted themselves to the apostles' teaching and to fellowship, to the breaking of bread and to prayer. Everyone was filled with awe at the many wonders and signs performed by the apostles. All the believers were together and had everything in common. They sold property and possessions to give to anyone who had need. Every day they continued to meet together in the temple courts. They broke bread in their homes and ate together with glad and sincere hearts, praising God and enjoying the favour of all the people. And the Lord added to their number daily those who were being saved."* (Acts 2:42-47)

Every single time I read those words; my heart begins to pound as I anticipate what that must have been like. Then I wonder, I ponder, and I long for the day when it might be like that again; a day when religion is finally sent back to the hell from which it came; a day when the community of faith which Jesus died to establish re-emerges in our midst with Jesus and His mission in the centre.

In the previous chapter I talked about our devotion to the Apostles' teaching, which for us is the New Testament, and how important it was for us to connect with all that Jesus did and taught and then passed on to the Apostles. In this chapter I want us to begin exploring a much more challenging devotion – one which takes a lifetime to do really well – but one which so defined this new Christian community. I am talking about their devotion to fellowship.

The Greek word translated as *fellowship* is *koinonia* and in Acts chapter 2 we encounter this word for the first time in the New Testament. This word *fellowship* has been used outside the confines of the church in our modern era – but it shouldn't have been. This word is a Christian word because this fellowship is the unique fellowship we have together in Christ. This is far more than a casual association, a club membership or just having your name on an organisation's roll. Koinonia fellowship is God-ordained, Christ-centred and Spirit-led. Koinonia only exists where the church exists, and it speaks to the heart of this new movement which began over 2,000 years ago.

This radical concept of fellowship and interdependence flies in the face of the individualism which dominates our society and that only highlights our need to re-connect with the true nature of the church. For millions of Christians today across the world, church life consists of a Sunday worship service and that's all - and even for those who are also involved in a small group of some kind, the true purpose and importance of that small group is not fully understood by many.

Now I firmly believe in the tremendous value of communal celebration and worship on Sunday, or any day, and I believe that solid teaching times are crucial for depth and strength. But you simply cannot read the New Testament and come away thinking that group gatherings in an auditorium once a week are the sum total of what the church is supposed to be. In fact, such gatherings, which have been the primary expression of the Christian church across much of the world for generations, can't be found in their current form anywhere in the New Testament, the foundational document upon which the church stands!

Let's look more closely now at this wonderful concept, captured by the Greek word *koinonia*. This word appears 19 times in the New Testament and this is the first time. It literally means *common* or *communal* and it signifies a close relationship, a sharing together, a participation, an intimacy. The word may only appear once in the passage we read from Acts 2, but the concept of koinonia runs through almost every sentence of this wonderful description of the church. Look closer with me:

> *"They devoted themselves ... to fellowship [koinonia] .. All the believers were together [koinonia] and had everything in common. [koinonia] Every day they continued to meet together [koinonia]... They broke bread in their homes [koinonia] and ate together [koinonia] with glad and sincere hearts ..."*

At the very heart of this new community of faith was *koinonia*: rich, personal, intimate, daily fellowship. What brought them together in this close bond of fellowship? It wasn't sport, music, hobbies, race, gender, jobs, economics, education, personalities or social status. In fact, nothing in this world created that special 'togetherness.' What brought them together was their shared life in Jesus Christ. This fellowship wasn't merely a social activity, shooting the breeze or hanging out together. Not that there's anything wrong with that, and that is often the starting point of true koinonia fellowship. We just need to accept that socialising isn't what the Bible portrays as fellowship.

Fellowship also isn't a place or a description of a group. We can call our Congregation a 'Christian Fellowship' but that does not guarantee that *koinonia* is actually taking place. It's more than a place and it's more than an event. Fellowship is our common, shared life in Jesus Christ. Fellowship is not a label – it's an experience. As John reminds us:

> *"We proclaim to you what we have seen and heard, so that you also may have fellowship with us. And our fellowship is with the Father and with his Son, Jesus Christ." (1 John 1:3)*

Any gathering of the church that leaves Jesus out is not *koinonia*, it's not true fellowship. For something to qualify as fellowship, the manifest presence of Christ has to be evident. True fellowship always begins with God. In the book of Acts they were called 'believers.' The glue that brings us together, holds us together, and keeps us together is Jesus Christ and our faith and belief in Him and His finished work of salvation. Look at what the Apostle Paul says about what happened to you when your eyes were opened to the reality of your Salvation in Christ.

> *Consequently, you are no longer foreigners and aliens, but fellow citizens with God's people and members of God's household, built on the foundation of the apostles and prophets, with Christ Jesus himself as the chief cornerstone. In him the whole building is joined together and rises to become a holy temple in the Lord. And in him you too are being built together to become a dwelling in which God lives by his Spirit.*
> *(Ephesians 2:19-22)*

When we become believers, our eyes are opened to the union we have with Jesus Christ; we recognise that we are part of God's family and as such, we become aware of a whole household of brothers and sisters. When we have fellowship with Jesus Christ, the dynamic of that relationship is meant to outflow into many relationships – into fellowship with each other.

> *If we walk in the light, as He is in the light, we have fellowship one with another. (1 John 1:7)*

So, in this modern era, is it even possible to experience this close, caring community like we see in the early church? What keeps this passage in Acts 2 from being a fairy tale from a lost era - an idealistic dream - instead of a 21st century reality? Can this imperfect group of forgiven believers really live together in community and intimacy? The Bible says we can.

God has designed us for closeness in the church Jesus promised to build and He wants us to make the effort to be together as often as we can. Being together is God's way of building *koinonia* in practical, visible, and tangible ways in the church. The New Testament stresses our involvement in this 'together' dynamic with a key truth captured in the recurring phrase 'one another'.

Just in case we miss the importance of fellowship and relating to each other, there are over thirty-five 'one another' statements in the New Testament. As you read them now, don't let them be 'theology' or 'doctrine' or a dry list in a book. I want you to imagine what these concepts could actually look like and feel like in your life and in the lives of those around you who claim to be your brothers and sisters in Christ.

I want you to dream about the kind of church we will be when all these statements are actually observations of who we are – rather than who we might like to be. Here are just some of the 'one another' statements from the Bible:

> Fellowship with one another - 1 John 1:5-7
> Confess your sins to one another - James 5:16
> Offer hospitality to one another - 1 Peter 4:9
> Clothe yourselves with humility toward one another - 1 Peter 5:5
> Do not lie to one another - Colossians 3:9

- > Comfort and encourage one another - 1 Thess.4:18
- > Spur one another to good deeds - Hebrews 10:24
- > Do not slander one another - James 4:1
- > Do not grumble at one another - James 5:9
- > Agree with one another - 1 Corinthians 1:10
- > Serve one another - 1 Corinthians 9:19 - 2 Corinthians 4:5
- > Have equal concern for one another - 1 Corinthians 12:25
- > Do not be conceited, provoking and envying one another - Galatians 5:26
- > Restore one another – Galatians 6:1
- > Bear with one another – Ephesians 4:2 – Colossians 3:13
- > Be kind to one another – Ephesians 4:32 – 1 Thess. 5:15
- > Sing to one another – Ephesians 5:19-20
- > Submit to one another – Ephesians 5:21
- > Wash one another's feet – John 13:14
- > Live in peace with one another – Romans 12:16 - 1 Thessalonians 5:13
- > Honour one another - Romans 12:10 - Philippians 2:3
- > Stop judging one another - Romans 14:13
- > Accept one another - Romans 15:7
- > Teach and admonish one another - Romans 15:14 - Colossians 3:16
- > Greet one another with a holy kiss - Romans 16:16 - 1 Corinthians 16:20
- > Love one another - John 13:34-35

Now, let me ask you something: Can all these 'one anothers' happen in just one worship service each week? No, of course they can't. That list itself demands a community of faith which shares its life together, just as they did when the church was born!

Sunday worship gatherings have a purpose. That's where our congregation gathers together in celebration and worship; to receive teaching; to celebrate communion; to pray and to share some fellowship. It is certainly not meant to be the only thing that happens each week for those who belong to the family of God. But being the church consists of so much more than that weekly get together.

Just imagine if we had only spent an hour or two once a week with our own families all those years we were together. What kind of relationship would we have with each other? How close would we be? How united in purpose would we be? How loved, appreciated and encouraged would we feel? How much would we be able to give to one another? How much would we even know each other? So it is with the family of God; the community of faith; the church. Without the willingness to be involved in the lives of others, we will simply not grow and ever become the wondrous miracle the church is meant to be.

Ok, that's the easy part! Essential as it is to identify the need (some don't even bother doing that) ... the really hard part is addressing that need by making different choices to the ones we've made in the past. That's the only way things change. That's the only way anything can improve or grow or mature or become more fruitful – by people deciding to make different choices. Those choices could be as simple as deciding to invite someone from your church to your place for a meal, so you can get to know them and their story and grow closer to them in their spiritual journey in Christ. Then invite someone different next time. Maybe make it a monthly thing. How hard could that be? It is not difficult to maintain fellowship, but it does require a commitment, or it just won't happen.

If everyone in every congregation decided to spend quality *koinonia* time together by phone or in person where possible, the Spirit of God would move through the church in this nation like a fire! If hosting a meal is too much for you, then a cup of tea and a biscuit for morning tea or afternoon tea is more than enough reason to gather together and give God an opportunity to show you what *koinonia* fellowship really feels like! You could even meet downtown for a cuppa at a café if you are not comfortable hosting people at home.

There are many aspects to being the church, but at the centre of them all – at the very heart of this organic, dynamic miracle of God, is *koinonia* – real fellowship: a dynamic, Spirit-led, gospel-centred, relational community. From the moment the church was born, we have been presented with a choice every day of our lives: relationship or religion. Every morning as your feet hit the floor and you begin a brand-new day, you have that same choice before you: relationship or religion. Our relationship with God and each other is what defines us as His people, His disciples, His church and if those relationships are growing, deepening and strengthening, then so will the church. God guarantees it.

Do we want the church to impact the community around us? Do we want to see God adding to our number daily like He did when all this began? Some people should answer no, to be honest, because some people might be comfortable with church the way it is - the way they have experienced for many years. But those who answer yes and genuinely want to see the Lord add to our number, must face the challenge God is presenting to us. If we want a different outcome, we need to make different choices. There's nothing very spiritual about that truth, but when applied to spiritual matters like the spread of the gospel and the health of the church, the outcome will be life-changing as the community around us is transformed by the power of God.

How devoted are you to fellowship, to *koinonia*, to the community of faith which Jesus promised to build, not the institution which man has built in Jesus' name? May God help you to answer that question as we work our way through this book. My prayer is that we will all have the courage to make some different choices and thereby become the answers to our own prayers for our community and our nation.

CHAPTER TEN
Giving the Church back to God

Throughout this book I have issued the challenge over and over again to stop 'going to church' and start 'being the church.' In fact, the phrase 'going to church' runs contrary to everything we learn about the church from the New Testament. The church is neither a destination nor an event. The church is not a particular building and nor is the church a particular gathering of people. Church is the collective word describing all the disciples of Jesus Christ who have been called to join His mission to advance the Kingdom of heaven on earth.

There's no building, denomination, creed or confession which can define or confine the church which Jesus is building. There are no boundaries to this church. There is no calendar which defines when we are the church and when we are not. We are the church seven days a week and every day is the Lord's Day!

Now we've been looking at the last part of Acts chapter 2 which gives us that beautiful and powerful snapshot of what the church Jesus promised to build looked like when it began and how it remained for many generations, and I hope we never stop examining our roots. In this chapter, I want us to fast forward to Acts 17 and take a glimpse at the impact this church and the disciples of Jesus had on the world, the same impact we will have on the world when we stop 'going to church,' stop perpetuating religion - and start living out the calling and relationship we have been given in Christ.

> *When Paul and his companions had passed through Amphipolis and Apollonia, they came to Thessalonica, where there was a Jewish synagogue. As was his custom, Paul went into the synagogue, and on three Sabbath days he reasoned with them from the Scriptures, explaining and proving that the Messiah had to suffer and rise from the dead. "This Jesus I am proclaiming to*

you is the Messiah," he said. Some of the Jews were persuaded and joined Paul and Silas, as did a large number of God-fearing Greeks and quite a few prominent women. But other Jews were jealous; so they rounded up some bad characters from the marketplace, formed a mob and started a riot in the city.

They rushed to Jason's house in search of Paul and Silas in order to bring them out to the crowd. But when they did not find them, they dragged Jason and some other believers before the city officials, shouting: "These men who have caused trouble all over the world have now come here, and Jason has welcomed them into his house. They are all defying Caesar's decrees, saying that there is another king, one called Jesus." (Acts 17:1-7)

What a tribute to Paul and Silas, to be referred to as the people, *"who have been turning the world upside down .."* (v.6) Wherever Paul went, things happened. Souls were saved, people took sides, fights broke out, feelings were stirred, decisions were made and lines were drawn. Paul didn't just slip into town, hold a few quiet meetings, enjoy some good home cooking, pick up a generous love offering and slip back out of town again without anyone knowing or caring that he had been there! Paul turned the place upside down! But how? How did the early disciples turn the world upside down? What was the secret to their success?

We already know from Acts 2 that the foundation of this new community was, in large part, the cause of their success. Their devotion to the Apostle's teaching, to fellowship, breaking of bread, prayer and worship became the bedrock upon which Jesus began building His church, all the time under the guidance of His empowering Spirit. But as this new church grew and moved out into the wider community and gained some more experience, there were four other important observations I would like to make which explains why their impact on the world was so significant and lasted so long. Firstly, they turned the world upside down because they possessed a power which was not their own. Paul explained this clearly in his first letter to the Corinthians:

> *When I came to you, I did not come with eloquence or human wisdom as I proclaimed to you the testimony about God. For I resolved to know nothing while I was with you except Jesus Christ and him crucified. I came to you in weakness with great fear and trembling. My message and my preaching were not with wise and persuasive words, but with a demonstration of the Spirit's power... (1 Corinthians 2:1-4)*

The Apostle Paul did not rely on persuasive arguments, human rhetoric, eloquence or man's wisdom; he did not come with fancy language; he did not come as a Christian salesman; he did not come with clever marketing pitches to get the people to make a profession of faith; he did not use gimmicks; he did not rely on his personal ability. Paul came to them, *"in weakness with great fear and trembling."*

When Paul considered on the one hand his weakness and limitations and on the other hand the importance of the message, he recognized it was going to take a supernatural work of God to achieve anything at all through him. It was not Paul's ability but the Holy Spirit's ability and Paul's availability that made things happen. Paul did not trust in his own natural talents. He later wrote:

> *"Not that we are competent in ourselves to claim anything for ourselves, but our competence comes from God."*
> *(2 Corinthians 3:5)*

Only God the Holy Spirit can convict, convince and transform the human heart. Paul was the proclaimer; the Holy Spirit was the persuader. Paul gave the invitation; the Holy Spirit drew people into the church. Paul recognized the Holy Spirit's power. His preaching carried conviction because of the power of the Spirit – not because of the quality of his preaching. Personality will not turn the world upside down. Money will not turn the world upside down. Organization will not turn the world upside down. Ordinary men and women filled with the power of the

Spirit of God can and will turn the world upside down! The Holy Spirit is present in every believer, prominent in some believers, but He was pre-eminent in those early believers when the church was born and it's from them, we need to learn where the true power of ministry comes from at all times. 'Being the church' will continue to be an unrealized dream if we do not give the Holy Spirit His rightful place at the helm of our lives and His church! We have to give the church back to God. We have to loosen our grip on our programs and plans and let the Holy Spirit lead us daily like He did when the church was born.

Sadly, for many believers, the Trinity has become the 'Father, Son and Holy Scripture.' I love the Bible. I have spent most of my life reading it, studying it, preaching from it and encouraging people to embrace God's Word within it. But I also respect what the Bible is and what it is not. Without the active presence of the Holy Spirit, the Bible is the most confusing book in the world and potentially, the most dangerous! Wars have been fought over this book because people have read it without the Holy Spirit's guidance. We have to be very careful. The Bible will not give us detailed instructions about how the church should operate and be structured in the 21st century. But the Holy Spirit will - and He will use many wonderful Scriptures in that process.

> *We just need to make sure we don't end up trusting a book which the early church didn't have, more than we trust the Holy Spirit Whom they did have.*

Secondly, they turned the world upside down through prayer. For every problem the early church encountered - their first response was to pray. They were confident in the power and effectiveness of prayer. You can see this all the way through the book of Acts. (4:17,18, 23, 24 and Acts 12:1-5, 6,7). Satan might have walled them in and surrounded them at times, but He could never roof them in. They always got through to God in prayer. All too often we pray when there's nothing else we can do - but Jesus wants us to pray before we do anything at all. Prayer does not equip us for the greater works: prayer *is* the greater work.

Prayer is not an escape from responsibility, it is our response to God's ability. The early church brought everything to God in prayer: their frustrations, their feelings, their enemies, their friends, their failures, hopes, dreams, fears and their praise for His grace and favour and victory. Prayer was not a ministry, it was part of their very personalities and their lives. Prayer was not something they did, it was how they lived – and the results were obvious.

For many of us, prayer is just a component of our Christian life; a ministry within the church – but for the early church it was an integral part of daily life. Talking to God in prayer was as natural as talking to each other. It was also absolutely essential. So much of the leading of the Holy Spirit actually came in answer to the prayers of the disciples! Prayer doesn't inform God – it transforms us! God knows everything already – even the prayers we haven't thought of yet! Prayer humbles us before God; it reminds us that He is God and we are not; it removes the pride, arrogance and misplaced confidence we may have in the flesh as we confess our need of God. Prayer is powerful and effective because it crucifies the flesh and releases the Spirit of God in us to do the work of God!

Thirdly, these early disciples turned the world upside down because they preached Christ crucified. Do you remember that very first sermon from Peter when the church was born on the day of Pentecost? Here is an excerpt:

> *"Fellow Israelites, listen to this: Jesus of Nazareth was a man accredited by God to you by miracles, wonders and signs, which God did among you through him, as you yourselves know. This man was handed over to you by God's deliberate plan and foreknowledge; and you, with the help of wicked men, put him to death by nailing him to the cross. But God raised him from the dead, freeing him from the agony of death, because it was impossible for death to keep its hold on him." (Acts 2:22-24)*

The all-consuming desire of the early church was to preach Christ crucified and introduce others to the risen, living Lord Jesus. This was their highest priority. This was their calling. This was their purpose. Teaching and preaching Jesus Christ and bringing people into a saving knowledge of Christ was why the church existed. This is what being the church looks like. If Christ is not in the centre of everything; if preaching and living the gospel is not our highest priority, our greatest passion and our main strategic purpose, then we are 'being' something other than the church.

The institutional church we see in the world today has taken up many noble causes and, as citizens of the earth, most of those causes are worthy of our time, effort, money and passion. But none of those causes actually define the church. None of those causes can ever rise above our basic purpose which is to preach Christ crucified, risen and coming again and introduce people to our living Lord and Saviour and call them to embrace His free gift of salvation as His disciples. When that single priority and defining purpose is overtaken by some other passion or cause, we stop being the church that we see in the book of Acts; we stop being the church Jesus is building and we start being something else, something far less.

I recently went online and started looking at church websites across Australia and around the world. I wanted to see how central Jesus Christ was and more importantly, the gospel message of 'Christ crucified' which the Apostles preached every day of their lives. I certainly had my eyes opened. It was a very enlightening exercise indeed. It was also the most depressing thing I have experienced for some time. The vast majority of church websites I visited highlighted service times, location, personnel, lists of ministry programs and activities. Some of them had a catchy mission or vision statement somewhere and some of those had a gospel focus of sorts – but nowhere was that unpacked and explained. If preaching Christ crucified lies at the very core of the church Jesus is building, you would never know it from most church websites I visited.

There is a 'Why Jesus?' link on the home page of my current congregation and that takes people to a page which outlines who Jesus is and why He is central to who we are and what we do. At the end of that page is another link: 'What is the Gospel?' On this page the whole gospel of Jesus Christ is unpacked and explained. Tragically, I could find nothing like these pages on the one hundred plus Church websites I looked at.

Preaching, sharing and living the gospel must be our highest priority and our defining purpose as the church. If that is not obvious to those within the church and those outside looking on, then we have lost our key distinctive and allowed lots of other worthwhile activities and priorities to overshadow the very reason we are here! It's like KFC running a marketing program and talking about everything except fried chicken! What would be the point of that? What is the point of any Christian ministry which does not have the life, death, resurrection and mission of Christ front and centre and the primary focus of everything they do and say? Being the church will always involve a return to the gospel in every aspect of church life.

Finally, these first disciples turned the world upside down because they were prepared to pay the price. Many of the early disciples of Christ were martyred for their service to the Lord. They rejoiced that they were counted worthy to suffer for the cause of Christ – even if that meant their own death. The measure of the importance of Christ is manifested in the lengths to which you will go to make Him known to others. If it meant jail or death to the early church, so be it. They were not going to stop teaching and preaching about Jesus Christ. The cause was greater than life itself. They went to extremes to make Christ known. It does not take great men and women to do great things; it only takes committed and called men and women. John Wesley once said:

> *"If I had 300 men who feared nothing but God, hated nothing but sin, and were determined to know nothing among mankind but Jesus Christ, and Him crucified, I would set the world on fire."*

The early church got involved in the cause of Christ; they took up His mission and committed their lives to its fulfilment. We must get involved in that same mission to truly make an impact. They were completely surrendered to the cause of Christ, and they knew that 'being the church' was a complete lifestyle commitment.

In the book of Revelation, we are told how the enemy of God, Satan, the prince of darkness, is overcome by us. Are you familiar with this verse? Do you even know you are able to triumph over the devil? Of course, you can. Jesus made that possible, and we get to bring that victory into our daily lives. How? Here's how:

"They triumphed over him by the blood of the Lamb and by the word of their testimony; they did not love their lives so much as to shrink from death." (Revelation 12:11)

This is a call to arms for the modern church. We overcome evil by the blood of the Lamb (Christ crucified!), the word of our testimony (preaching and living the gospel) and by going all the way, even to the point of death, if required. God is not calling us all to literally die for Him - there would be nobody left to carry on His mission. But God is certainly calling us all to have the same attitude, the same commitment, the same determination and faith as someone who is fully prepared to die for Christ.

Do you want to be part of those who are described as, *"These people who have been turning the world upside down."* That's who the church is supposed to be. If we are committed to truly being the church, then we will be people who turn the world upside down. As radical as that may sound, never forget that all this world-changing stuff always begins with the basics: devoting ourselves to the Apostles teaching; devoting ourselves to rich, koinonia fellowship; sharing meals together; praying together; worshipping together; and committing ourselves to the mission of Jesus Christ together.

Our forebears turned the world upside down in ways we may only dream of, and yet, we have everything they had and more! There is nothing stopping us having the same impact they had – and even greater. *Come, Holy Spirit, teach us, guide us, empower us to be the church Jesus promised to build.*

CHAPTER ELEVEN
The Weeds of Unbelief

As we continue to open ourselves to the Holy Spirit in our study of what it means to truly be the church, I want to address the greatest threat to us fulfilling our calling as disciples of Jesus Christ. Let me stress first of all that the productiveness or the fruitfulness of a word that God spoke does not validate whether it was from God or not. That is the clear message of the parable of the sower and why we are presented with four different kinds of soil. Three of these soils were no good but the seed was still authentic - it just didn't bear fruit. The seed is never the problem. The fault is never in what God says – the fruitfulness is always determined by the soil.

Many people make the mistake here of thinking that we judge a tree by its fruit and that's absolutely right. But they will wrongly assume that we know whether this was a word from God or not by the fruit. That is not always the case. You will remember that Jesus once spoke into the lives of ten lepers and healed them all. But only one leper had a character change enough to return and give thanks. Does that mean the other nine were falsely healed? No, God's word is not validated by what we do with it. God is never on trial by what I do - I am.

> *The seed falling among the thorns refers to someone who hears the word, but the worries of this life and the deceitfulness of wealth choke the word, making it unfruitful. (Matthew 13:22)*

If you are a gardener, you will know that if you stop caring for your garden – then it will not be long before the weeds are up to your knees and the good plants are not even visible. We will always have weeds because the seeds are deposited by birds and sometimes the soil we bring in to top up our garden already has seeds in it. We plant good seeds and seedlings but other seeds compete and very often the weeds will grow in times of neglect more than the good plants because many of them require less moisture and will always overtake a neglected garden. Herein lies the challenge for each of us. God's word comes to us – this good seed which we receive into the soil of our heart. But we have this other word; and this other idea; and over here we have this disappointment; or this criticism; or this complaint; or this doubt or fear. We've got all these other seeds that are vying for the same nutrients. They all want to germinate and take root in our heart: the cares of this world; the worries of this life; various other burdens or concerns and especially the busyness of life - all compete with the good seed.

Let me just give you a quote here for your fridge door: *Busyness is artificial significance.* The enemy works to expand our busyness to increase our cares and worries so he can then plant seeds that compete with the Word of God. By far the greatest 'weed' of all and the most pervasive, is unbelief.

> *A man in the crowd answered, "Teacher, I brought you my son, who is possessed by a spirit that has robbed him of speech. Whenever it seizes him, it throws him to the ground. He foams at the mouth, gnashes his teeth and becomes rigid. I asked your disciples to drive out the spirit, but they could not."*
>
> *"You unbelieving generation," Jesus replied, "how long shall I stay with you? How long shall I put up with you? Bring the boy to me." (Mark 9:17-19)*

Now in the NKJV and the RSV translations of the Bible, Jesus replies, *"You faithless generation."* In the NIV which I am using here and the NASB it is translated, *"You unbelieving generation."* This is one of those times when the translation makes all the difference and I'm a little annoyed that two of the most popular Bible translations in the world today have used this word *faithless* because that is not what it says. The literal word in the Greek is translated *unbelief* and those two things are definitely not the same. Let me explain.

Simply put, unbelief is not the absence of faith, it is merely the presence of unbelief. There is a difference. Later in verse 24 this man says, *"I do believe, help me overcome my unbelief."* The problem here is you can have more than one seed growing in your garden but to say it's a faithless garden is not accurate. There is faith in the garden. There is good seed in the garden. To call it faithless is not true. There's just unbelief there as well.

Over the years I have heard people who struggle to embrace the gospel say things like, *"Well, I have more of an intellectual bent."* What they are really saying is they have an unbelieving bent, and that's nothing to be proud of. I have it on good authority that God is pretty smart; He is very intelligent; I think they call it *omniscient* – which means He is the only genuine 'know-it-all' - and yet God's intellect and knowledge doesn't interfere with His faith. So, if my intellect and knowledge is affecting my faith, obviously what I know is wrong and I allow my garden to be filled with seeds that compete with what God has said. They compete with the Truth.

True faith gives you access to your single greatest source of intelligence. I believe in the days ahead we are going to see the greatest intellectualism mankind has ever seen and it will come out of faith. Here's another one for your fridge door: *We don't believe because we understand - we understand because we believe.* Faith gives us access to a level of understanding which you will never get through human reasoning. Ok, back to Mark's gospel:

> *"You unbelieving generation," Jesus replied, "how long shall I stay with you? How long shall I put up with you? Bring the boy to me." So, they brought him. When the spirit saw Jesus, it immediately threw the boy into a convulsion. He fell to the ground and rolled around, foaming at the mouth. (Mark 9:19-20)*

The evil spirit obviously did this in front of the disciples and it worked. If you can create enough disturbance with what you see in the natural, it can interfere with what you see in the Spirit. You see faith doesn't deny a problem's existence - it just denies the problem a place of influence.

> *Jesus asked the boy's father, "How long has he been like this?"*
>
> *"From childhood," he answered. "It has often thrown him into fire or water to kill him. But if you can do anything, take pity on us and help us."*

> *"'If you can'?" said Jesus. "Everything is possible for one who believes." Immediately the boy's father exclaimed, "I do believe; help me overcome my unbelief!" When Jesus saw that a crowd was running to the scene, he rebuked the impure spirit. "You deaf and mute spirit," he said, "I command you, come out of him and never enter him again." The spirit shrieked, convulsed him violently and came out. The boy looked so much like a corpse that many said, "He's dead." But Jesus took him by the hand and lifted him to his feet, and he stood up." (Mark 9:21-28)*

There are several things we could note in this story, but I want to focus on just one here. Just picture your garden again. You have these good plants you have nurtured from a seed but in between those plants are others you did not put there. They just appeared and all of the plants are now competing for air, water, sunlight and nutrients. There's this battle going on because when you water the garden you also water the weeds. Nobody has invented a watering system that only waters the good plants!

The point I'm trying to make is the water of God's presence waters all seeds. Whatever seed is in the soil will become visible in the presence of the Lord. The good seed and the weeds will both emerge in the presence of God and that is actually a good thing. You don't want hidden weeds doing damage under the ground or hiding somewhere in your garden. You really need everything to be revealed and God is always revealing what's in our hearts – whether we like what is revealed or not.

Let me illustrate this concept that the presence of the Lord causes all seeds to grow by pointing you to the Last Supper. This is the most intense and intimate moment ever between Jesus and His twelve closest colleagues. They would have been able to feel it in the air. The presence of God would have been so intense. Something is about to happen, Jesus knows He's about to go to the cross but His disciples just feel the anticipation – they are in this intense moment of Divine Presence, this intimate moment. We see John with his head on Jesus' chest; Peter announcing he will never deny Jesus and we have Judas walking out of the room to betray the Lord. All the seeds are watered in the presence of God – the good ones and the bad ones. They all manifest (become visible) in these moments. You just need wisdom to recognize when the Lord is bringing something to the surface and in that moment, He has given you the grace to deal with it quickly and thoroughly. Throughout our lives we will discover all kinds of things planted in the soil of our heart. We've got the word of the Lord over our life, but like this guy in Mark 9, we believe, but we also struggle with unbelief.

We've wrongly thought that the answer to this challenge is to have more faith. Jesus rejected that notion when He said faith just the size of a mustard seed could move mountains! That's not just a nice, warm, fuzzy illustration. It's not a motivational line. It's a clear statement of fact: something this small can move something that big. So, you see the problem is not the size of our faith – the problem is we have other plants in our garden and those thorns and weeds can overpower the good seed if we don't tend to our garden regularly.

There are lots of different weeds in our gardens at home which compete with the good plants we want to nurture and grow. In the same way there can be lots of different weeds in our heart which compete with God's word every day. However, I want to suggest to you that most weeds we contend with in our hearts come from the same single species – the same source: unbelief. In fact, I would say that unbelief is the cause of most of our struggles. The Bible and our own experiences confirm that the primary sin that robs us of the fullness of God's promises, power and manifest presence is the sin of unbelief.

If you remain diligent in the garden of your heart and you continually identify and remove those weeds of unbelief then all those wonderful promises of God will, over time, become your experience: *"I will keep you in perfect peace ... You will be able to do all things through Christ who strengthens you ... Ask anything in my name and I will do it for you."*

The Word of God will produce fruit because it has within it the power to fulfil His promises. All it needs is fertile, deep, rich, open, co-operative soil – all of which equates to a believing, teachable, receptive heart.

By faith we may embrace all the wonderful promises of God, but deep down we struggle to really believe they are for us, right here and now. Let's look at some of the opening words of the Apostle Paul in his letter to the Ephesians:

Praise be to the God and Father of our Lord Jesus Christ, who has blessed us in the heavenly realms with every spiritual blessing in Christ. (Ephesians 1:3)

If you are a disciple of Christ, you now have everything in Christ, but if you don't really believe that is true and don't act on that belief every day - then you will never experience it.

For he chose us in him before the creation of the world to be holy and blameless in his sight. (Ephesians 1:4)

He has already done that. Any attempt on our part to 'become' holy in His sight is futile and we just need to repent of that sin of unbelief. Unbelief gives rise to every other sin in life, from the Garden of Eden till now.

Why do believers still covet, steal, lie or commit adultery? It is because they don't believe they already have everything in Christ; you don't have to strive to be accepted in Christ; you don't have to try to attain God's holiness by your religious performance; you don't need drugs to find peace with God; you don't need to manipulate people into liking you. Just know and believe that you are loved by God Himself.

Unbelief is really the mother and father of all sins. Every other sin that we feel bad about is our futile attempt to earn the things that God has already freely given us. God said to Adam and Eve: *"I give you everything in abundance. It is all good."* Then the serpent said, *"God is withholding something from you. If you really want to live, then in addition to all that God has given you, you need to take this forbidden fruit."*

Taking the fruit was not Adam and Eve's first sin. Not believing what God had told them was their first sin. Unbelief was the first sin and the cause of almost every other sin!

> *In love he predestined us to be adopted as his sons and daughters through Jesus Christ, in accordance with his pleasure and will – to the praise of his glorious grace, which he has freely given us in the One he loves. (Ephesians 1:5-6)*

There is no more that we need. We just need to believe what we are told and step out and act as if it were true. We have all we need for our life in Jesus Christ; all we need for godliness; all we need for happiness; all we need for an authentic life; all we need for our church to become the church Christ promised to build. If we have prepared good, rich, open, receptive soil; if we meditate on the fact that we already have everything in Christ and live like that fact is true, then we will begin to experience all that God has given us and promised us. If we don't, we won't.

Our lives are full of all kinds of sins, and we tend to put them in different categories. We repent of them as we feel convicted, but until we repent of the primary sin of unbelief, our lives will never work, and we will go on committing many other sins which flow from our unbelief.

God told Abraham that he and Sarah would have a son. Abraham's unbelief caused him to try to help out by having a son with Hagar. He then had to repent of his second sin as well as the primary sin of unbelief.

Throughout my many years in ministry, I have endeavoured to showcase our complete freedom in Christ; that we are ok with God; and that His life is given to us freely - we never have to earn it. Why have I done that? Why has this seemed like a cracked record? There are several reasons. Firstly, it's New Testament truth, and we all need to hear it often.

Secondly, I want those to whom I preach or write to become increasingly more free, full of joy and confidence, experiencing more and more of the abundant life which is theirs in Christ.

The third reason is that when we really believe and act on these truths, sin won't be an issue. Romans 6 says we are no longer slaves to sin. Hebrews 10 tells us that we have been made holy and presented to God, perfect in Christ. Paul sums it up well in his letter to the Romans.

> *It was not through law that Abraham and his offspring received the promise that he would be heir of the world, but through the righteousness that comes by faith. For if those who live by law are heirs, faith has no value and the promise is worthless, because law brings wrath. And where there is no law there is no transgression. Therefore, the promise comes by faith, so that it may be by grace. (Romans 4:13-16)*

The promise comes by faith so that it may be in accordance with grace. Grace says, *'You don't have to work for it – you get it free.'* If it's by faith, then anyone can do it. Religion says: *'You reach God's highest purposes if you are a good pray-er. You need to live a life of holiness and purity to reach spiritual maturity. You will only stand in the end-times army of God if you clean up your act.'*

No, no, no! You get it by believing what you've been told and acting on that, according to grace. Anybody can believe; you don't need super intelligence; you don't need to have the right connections; you don't need to be wealthy or good-looking. Anybody can believe God's Word. Jesus had a way of making it so simple it hits us in the face.

> *"The disciples asked Him: "What must we do to do the works of God?" Jesus told them: "This is the work of God – to believe in the One He sent." (John 6:28-29)*

This is our primary work – to believe in Jesus. If you want to work hard for God, then let that belief be translated into action: become the person you already are in Christ. Belief without action is not belief at all. Part of that work of faith is repenting of those actions by which we are trying to achieve for ourselves that God has already given us. That is why it is so crucial that we understand the full implications of God's grace and all that we have been given freely in Christ. We need to know deep in our hearts that we are OK not because of our own behaviour or our performance against a set of laws or requirements. We are OK because Jesus made us OK. *'Jesus plus nothing'* is our salvation and our life. That is the only solid foundation for building the church. God will remove any other.

In the final analysis, if our life is not working; if we are hurting, suffering physically, emotionally, spiritually, it's not because of our mother or father or employer or the Government or anyone else's sin against us – past, present or future – it's not even ultimately because of the secondary sins in our own life. Our problems arise from one primary sin: the sin of unbelief.

When we finally believe that we are totally, unconditionally loved, accepted and made holy before God and empowered by His free grace as given to us in Christ, then we will no longer be intimidated by anything - either from without or within - even our own sins and shortcomings. We can hand them all over to God, once and for all.

The Bible is the account of mankind's experiences with God. It is His story, rather than ours. God is the central character: Creator, Author, Hero and Finisher of this long narrative, and as the story unfolds, so does the revelation about God. From the beginning, He is a God of grace, choosing people and making promises to them, blessing them, and keeping His promises despite their failure. Such is His love that He always treats His people with dignity and respect, allowing them to respond to Him by their own choice. Those commended by God in Hebrews chapter 11 are the ones who chose to believe His word, take part in His plans, and see the fruit emerge in their lives.

> *Therefore, since we are surrounded by such a great cloud of witnesses, let us throw off everything that hinders and the sin that so easily entangles, and let us run with perseverance the race marked out for us. Let us fix our eyes on Jesus, the author and perfector of our faith, who for the joy set before him endured the cross, scorning its shame, and sat down at the right hand of the throne of God. Consider him who endured such opposition from sinful men, so that you will not grow weary and lose heart.*
> *(Hebrews 12:1-3)*

If we are to be fully equipped as the church; if we are to fulfill the mission of Christ on earth today; if we really want to be the church, then we need to tend the garden of our hearts every day and deal with those weeds of unbelief which the enemy of God places there every day. May we hear the words of Jesus afresh today: *"This is the work of God – to believe in the One He sent."* We already have everything we need to live an authentic, productive Christian life – it has already been given to us in Christ. Our task, if we want to truly be the church, is to believe that truth and then start walking in that reality.

CHAPTER TWELVE
Come, Holy Spirit

As important as it has been to embark upon this study and see the many areas we may like to revisit if we truly want to be the church, I want to just step back from the detail now and ask the key question: how? How was it possible for those first disciples to enjoy such incredible success and growth? Was there a secret to establishing a church which grew at such a phenomenal rate each and every year for two hundred years or more? Did they just follow a plan and tick off the tasks each day?

Did they simply decide one day that they would devote themselves to the Apostles teaching every day; share deep, rich *koinonia* fellowship every day; share meals with each other in their homes every day and worship together every day? Were these things simply on their 'to do' list or part of some strategic plan and the rest of this miracle just happened? Absolutely not.

We humans lack the capacity to discipline ourselves to follow a list of tasks for that long and God only blesses and grows what comes from our hearts. The rest is just works-based religion and we all know that God hates religion. What was it then that allowed our forebears to get it so right for so long and have such an incredible impact on the world? Actually, the correct question is not 'what,' but 'Who' made all this possible? This 'Who' is mentioned in almost every chapter in the book of Acts and in many chapters, multiple times. Of course, I am speaking about the Holy Spirit.

Everything about the early church which made it powerful, effective, real, world-changing and dynamic – was initiated and empowered the Holy Spirit. The disciples were responsible for discerning the presence of the Spirit; listening to the voice of the Spirit; and responding in obedience to the Spirit.

This should not surprise us, because the One Who birthed this miracle of the church, Jesus Christ, operated exactly the same way when He walked among us.

Long before the book of Acts and the birth of the church, Jesus Himself modelled this distinctive Spirit-led lifestyle to His disciples. Jesus Christ is the only perfect manifestation in history of the complete work of the Holy Spirit in and through a human being. Jesus was even begotten of the Holy Spirit. He is the only begotten Son of God. It was entirely by the Holy Spirit's power working in Mary that the Son of God was formed within her. Jesus also led a holy life and offered Himself without spot to God through the working of the Holy Spirit.

> *How much more shall the blood of Christ, who through the eternal Spirit offered Himself without spot to God, purge your conscience from dead works to serve the living God. (Hebrews 9:14)*

Jesus met and overcame temptations as other men and women may meet and overcome them - in the power of the Holy Spirit. Jesus was anointed and fitted for service by the Holy Spirit.

> *... how God anointed Jesus of Nazareth with the Holy Spirit and power, and how he went around doing good and healing all who were under the power of the devil, because God was with him. (Acts 10:38)*

> *Jesus returned to Galilee in the power of the Spirit, and news about him spread through the whole countryside. (Luke 4:14)*

In a similar way Jesus said this of Himself when speaking in the synagogue in Nazareth:

> *The Spirit of the Lord is on me, because he has anointed me to proclaim good news to the poor. He has sent me to proclaim freedom for the prisoners and recovery of sight for the blind, to set the oppressed free, to proclaim the year of the Lord's favour. (Luke 4:18-19)*

All these passages contain the one truth: it was by the anointing of the Holy Spirit that Jesus Christ was qualified for the service to which God had called Him. As He stood in the Jordan river after His baptism, the Holy Spirit descended and rested upon

Him like a dove, and it was then and there that He was anointed with the Holy Spirit and equipped for the service that lay ahead. Jesus received His equipping for service in the same way that we receive ours - by the Holy Spirit. Jesus was taught by the Spirit Who rested upon Him. The Spirit of God was the source of His wisdom, direction and power whilst He was on earth. This was prophesied many years beforehand by the prophet Isaiah:

> *The Spirit of the Lord will rest on him – the Spirit of wisdom and of understanding, the Spirit of counsel and of might, the Spirit of the knowledge and fear of the Lord – and he will delight in the fear of the Lord. He will not judge by what he sees with his eyes, or decide by what he hears with his ears (Isaiah 11:2-3)*

> *Here is my servant, whom I uphold, my chosen one in whom I delight; I will put my Spirit on him, and he will bring justice to the nations (Isaiah 17:1)*

Matthew tells us that this prophecy was fulfilled in Jesus of Nazareth (see Matthew 12:17-18). The Holy Spirit remained with Jesus in all His fullness and the words He spoke in consequence were the very words of God.

> *For the one whom God has sent speaks the words of God, for God[a] gives the Spirit without limit. (John 3:34)*

> *... until the day he was taken up to heaven, after giving instructions through the Holy Spirit to the apostles he had chosen. (Acts 1:2)*

This relates to the time after His resurrection and so we see Jesus still working in the power of the Holy Spirit even after His resurrection from the dead. Jesus performed His miracles here on earth in the power of the Holy Spirit.

> *... it is by the Spirit of God that I drive out demons...*
> *(Matthew 12:28)*

It was by the power of the Holy Spirit that Jesus was raised from the dead.

> *And if the Spirit of him who raised Jesus from the dead is living in you, he who raised Christ from the dead will also give life to your mortal bodies because of[a] his Spirit who lives in you. (Romans 8:11)*

Several things are plainly evident from this study of the work of the Holy Spirit in the earthy life of Jesus Christ: First of all, we see the completeness of His humanity. He lived, He thought, He worked, He taught, He conquered sin and won victories for God in the power of that very same Spirit Whom it is our privilege also to have with us.

Secondly, we see our own utter dependence upon the Holy Spirit. If it was in the power of the Holy Spirit that Jesus Christ, the only begotten Son of God, lived and worked, achieved and triumphed, how much more dependent are we upon the Spirit at every turn of our lives and in every phase of service and every experience of conflict with Satan and sin?

The third thing which is evident is the wondrous world of privilege, blessing, victory and conquest that is open to us. The same Spirit by which Jesus was originally begotten is within us so we can be 'begotten' again (born again) of Him.

The same Spirit by Whom Jesus offered Himself without spot or blemish to God is within us so we may also offer ourselves without spot or blemish to God. The same Spirit by Whom Jesus was anointed for service is within us so we also may be anointed for service. The same Spirit Who led Jesus every day of His life and ministry here on earth is ready to lead us today. The same Spirit Who taught Jesus and imparted to Him wisdom and understanding, counsel and might, knowledge and the fear of the Lord is here to do the same for us. Jesus Christ is our pattern (1 John 2:6), *"the first born among many brethren"* (Romans 8:29). Whatever He realised through the Holy Spirit – we too can realise today.

Now perhaps we can understand why the book of Acts is full of references to the Holy Spirit. The miracle of the church and its impact on the world came in direct proportion to the people's knowledge of and submission to the Spirit.

There are actually 45 verses in the book of Acts which highlight the work of the Holy Spirit. Without that moment-by-moment work of the Spirit of God, there would be no Acts of the Apostles; there would be no church. If we read through the book of Acts, we see for ourselves just how prominent the Holy Spirit was. In the very first chapter of Acts we find Jesus warning the disciples to not do anything until they have the Holy Spirit.

> *(Jesus) gave them this command: "Do not leave Jerusalem, but wait for the gift my Father promised, which you have heard me speak about. For John baptized with water, but in a few days, you will be baptized with the Holy Spirit …. You will receive power when the Holy Spirit comes on you; and you will be my witnesses in Jerusalem, and in all Judea and Samaria, and to the ends of the earth. (Acts 1:4-5,8)*

Why did Jesus tell them to wait? Because without the Holy Spirit we are aimless and dangerous; we are completely ineffective; we are powerless; we are disconnected from heaven and the power of God. All we have is religion and a man-made institution which is completely powerless to change the world. Jesus had taught these disciples so much over the previous three years and they had a lot of knowledge and experience. But the main thing He taught them was that He achieved nothing apart from the Holy Spirit. Everything in His ministry was in response to the Spirit's leading and empowering. The disciples knew that, so they waited for that power from on high before attempting anything in Jesus' name. If only the modern church would do the same. If only we would wait for that power from on high before we race off into our ministries and plans in Jesus' name. Here are all the other references to the Holy Spirit in the Book of Acts:

> *Brothers and sisters, the Scripture had to be fulfilled which the Holy Spirit spoke long ago through the mouth of David concerning Judas, who served as guide for those who arrested Jesus. (Acts 1:16)*

> *All of them were filled with the Holy Spirit and began to speak in other tongues as the Spirit enabled them. (Acts 2:4)*

In the last days, God says, I will pour out my Spirit on all people. Your sons and daughters will prophesy, your young men will see visions, your old men will dream dreams. Even on my servants, both men and women, I will pour out my Spirit in those days, and they will prophesy. (Acts 2:17-18)

Exalted to the right hand of God, he has received from the Father the promised Holy Spirit and has poured out what you now see and hear. (Acts 2:33)

Peter replied, "Repent and be baptized, every one of you, in the name of Jesus Christ for the forgiveness of your sins. And you will receive the gift of the Holy Spirit." (Acts 2:38)

Then Peter, filled with the Holy Spirit, said to them: "Rulers and elders of the people!" (Acts 4:8)

You spoke by the Holy Spirit through the mouth of your servant, our father David. (Acts 4:25a)

After they prayed, the place where they were meeting was shaken. And they were all filled with the Holy Spirit and spoke the word of God boldly. (Acts 4:31)

Then Peter said, "Ananias, how is it that Satan has so filled your heart that you have lied to the Holy Spirit and have kept for yourself some of the money you received for the land?" (Acts 5:3)

Peter said to her, "How could you agree to test the Spirit of the Lord?" (Acts 5:9)

We are witnesses of these things, and so is the Holy Spirit, whom God has given to those who obey him. (Acts 5:32)

Brothers, choose seven men from among you who are known to be full of the Spirit and wisdom. (Acts 6:3)

They chose Stephen, a man full of faith and of the Holy Spirit. (Acts 6:5)

They could not stand up against his wisdom or the Spirit by whom he spoke. (Acts 6:10)

... you are just like your ancestors: You always resist the Holy Spirit! (Acts 7:51)

Stephen, full of the Holy Spirit, looked up to heaven and saw the glory of God, and Jesus standing at the right hand of God. (Acts 7:55)

When they arrived, they prayed for the new believers there that they might receive the Holy Spirit, because the Holy Spirit had not yet come on any of them; they had simply been baptized in the name of the Lord Jesus. Then Peter and John placed their hands on them, and they received the Holy Spirit. When Simon saw that the Spirit was given at the laying on of the apostles' hands, he offered them money and said, "Give me also this ability so that everyone on whom I lay my hands may receive the Holy Spirit. (Acts 8:15-19)

The Spirit told Philip, "Go to that chariot and stay near it." (Acts 8:29)

When they came up out of the water, the Spirit of the Lord suddenly took Philip away. (Acts 8:39a)

Jesus ... has sent me so that you may see again and be filled with the Holy Spirit. (Acts 9:17)

It [the church] was strengthened; and encouraged by the Holy Spirit, it increased in numbers. (Acts 9:31)

While Peter was still thinking about the vision, the Spirit said to him, "Simon, three men are looking for you." (Acts 10:19)

... God anointed Jesus of Nazareth with the Holy Spirit and power. (Acts 10:38)

While Peter was still speaking these words, the Holy Spirit came on all who heard the message. (Acts 10:44)

The circumcised believers who had come with Peter were astonished that the gift of the Holy Spirit had been poured out even on the Gentiles. (Acts 10:45)

Surely no one can stand in the way of theirfrom being baptized with water? They have received the Holy Spirit just as we have. (Acts 10:47)

The Spirit told me to have no hesitation about going with them. (Acts 11:12a)

As I began to speak, the Holy Spirit came on them as he had come on us at the beginning. Then I remembered what the Lord had said: "John baptized with water, but you will be baptized with the Holy Spirit." (Acts 11:15-16)

He was a good man, full of the Holy Spirit and faith, and a great number of people were brought to the Lord. (Acts 11:24)

One of them, named Agabus, stood up and through the Spirit predicted that a severe famine would spread over the entire Roman world. (Acts 11:28)

While they were worshipping the Lord and fasting, the Holy Spirit said, "Set apart for me Barnabas and Saul for the work to which I have called them." (Acts 13:2)

The two of them, sent on their way by the Holy Spirit, went down to Seleucia ... (Acts 13:4)

Then Saul, who was also called Paul, filled with the Holy Spirit, looked straight at Elymas and said, "You are a child of the devil." (Acts 13:9-10a)

The disciples were filled with joy and with the Holy Spirit. (Acts 13:52)

God, who knows the heart, showed that he accepted them by giving the Holy Spirit to them, just as he did to us. (Acts 15:8)

It seemed good to the Holy Spirit and to us not to burden you with anything beyond the following requirements. (Acts 15:28)

Paul and his companions travelled throughout the region of Phrygia and Galatia, having been kept by the Holy Spirit from preaching the word in the province of Asia. When they came to the border of Mysia, they tried to enter Bithynia, but the Spirit of Jesus would not allow them to. (Acts 16:6-7)

"Did you receive the Holy Spirit when you believed?" They answered, "No, we have not even heard that there is a Holy Spirit." (Acts 19:2)

When Paul placed his hands on them, the Holy Spirit came on them, and they spoke in tongues and prophesied. (Acts 19:6)

Compelled by the Spirit, I am going to Jerusalem, not knowing what will happen to me there. I only know that in every city the Holy Spirit warns me that prison and hardships are facing me. (Acts 20:22-23)

Keep watch over yourselves and all the flock of which the Holy Spirit has made you overseers. (Acts 20:28a)

Through the Spirit they urged Paul not to go on to Jerusalem." (Acts 21:4b)

How much clearer can it be? Everything Jesus did, was in direct response to the leading of the Holy Spirit. Everything the church which Jesus' birthed did, was empowered and guided by the Holy Spirit. The Holy Spirit was their constant guide. The Holy Spirit was their only source of discernment about what they should speak and what they should do every day. The Holy Spirit was the source of all their power, wisdom and truth. The Holy Spirit was the reason why anything they did actually bore fruit and impacted the world. Wherever the Holy Spirit moved and God's people responded, lives, families and communities were transformed.

The unprecedented success and impact of the early church was all due to the work of the Spirit of God. Nowhere else in history do we have such a powerful example of the transforming power of a group of ordinary people on the whole society around them. It was extraordinary and it all revolved around the work of the Holy Spirit. However, we must understand something about the Holy Spirit – He will not barge in and take over. The only reason the Holy Spirit was so powerful, so effective and so present in the life of Jesus is because Jesus chose to submit to the Spirit daily. Jesus could have spoken and acted on His own, but He chose to speak only the words His Father gave Him to speak, through the Spirit; He chose only to do what He saw the Father doing, which was revealed to Him by the Holy Spirit.

The primary reason the early church exploded across the world like a raging bushfire, capturing the hearts and lives of millions of people is because those early disciples made a choice to submit themselves to the Holy Spirit every single day and allowed the Spirit of Christ, the head of the church, to call all the shots – right down to their day-by-day instructions about where to minister and what to say!

For many years I have been pleading with my brothers and sisters in Christ and especially those in leadership in the Body of Christ to give the church back to God. The book of Acts shows us what the church will look like and be like whenever we have the courage to loosen our grip on what is not ours and never was. When we get over our demonic, irrational fear of the Holy Spirit and actually trust Him the way Jesus did and the way the early disciples did, then what we see in the life of Christ and the early church will become our reality.

Jesus said, *"I will build my church ..."* and there is only one way He can do that - directly and deliberately through His Spirit. When we let go of the reigns of the church we have built and let the Holy Spirit take the lead in every area of our lives and our ministry, then we will finally see the church *Jesus* is building and we will be writing our own book of Acts, and it will be just as powerful, just as confronting and just as mind-boggling as the first one written by Luke.

Jesus told His disciples to wait and not to go anywhere or do anything in His name until they received power from on high – until the Holy Spirit was released in their midst to guide them and empower this new church. Jesus knew what would happen if they raced off in their own strength and tried to save the world with nothing but hearts full of good intentions. They would have ended up with a powerless, ineffective, marginalized, shrinking, irrelevant church. Does that sound familiar? It should.

Perhaps it is time we burned all our church growth books, cancelled our 'how-to' seminars and just decided to heed Jesus' warning again. Maybe we need to shut down every ministry of the church we have built – close it all down – and wait in prayer, for as long as it takes, doing nothing else, until we receive that power from on high – until the Holy Spirit once again takes up the reigns of the church Jesus is building and directs our every word and action. A global pandemic provided most of that 'shutdown' for us recently, but my fear is that we have emerged on the other side not all that different to how we went in.

I wonder what might have happened when we emerged from that unprecedented ministry hiatus, had we all spent that time on our knees in prayer before God, asking that the post-pandemic church will be one led and empowered entirely by the Holy Spirit. I wonder what might have emerged if we had let go of all our plans and man-made visions of the church and allowed God to rebirth the Spirit-led church Jesus promised to build. My mind boggles as my heart pounds with anticipation of what might have been.

The bottom line is this – and it's embarrassingly simple: when you look at the life and ministry of Jesus during His time on earth; and the life and ministry of the early church He birthed, you cannot avoid the fact that the sovereign presence, power and moment-by-moment reality of the Holy Spirit is the only reason Jesus and the early disciples achieved anything at all. As we observe how these ordinary people, in partnership with the Holy Spirit, achieved so much; turning the whole world upside down, that should provide us with our strongest motivation and our greatest encouragement to follow their lead.

Do you remember when Peter and John healed the lame man at the temple gate and news spread and they found themselves dragged before the Sanhedrin to answer for actions? They testified to the power of the resurrected Christ and were scolded, threatened and sent on their way. What did they do next? Let me remind you and give you another glimpse into what being the church really looks like:

"On their release, Peter and John went back to their own people and reported all that the chief priests and the elders had said to them. When they heard this, they raised their voices together in prayer to God. "Sovereign Lord," they said, "you made the heavens and the earth and the sea, and everything in them. You spoke by the Holy Spirit through the mouth of your servant, our father David ... Indeed, Herod and Pontius Pilate met together with the Gentiles and the people of Israel in this city to conspire against your holy servant Jesus, whom you anointed. They did what your power and will had decided beforehand should happen.

Now, Lord, consider their threats and enable your servants to speak your word with great boldness. Stretch out your hand to heal and perform signs and wonders through the name of your holy servant Jesus. After they prayed, the place where they were meeting was shaken. And they were all filled with the Holy Spirit and spoke the word of God boldly.

All the believers were one in heart and mind. No one claimed that any of their possessions was their own, but they shared everything they had. With great power the apostles continued to testify to the resurrection of the Lord Jesus. And God's grace was so powerfully at work in them all." (Acts 4:23-33)

If we truly want to be the church, then we have to let it go; we have to give the church back to God as we allow the Holy Spirit His rightful place once again in our hearts, our committees, our conferences, our worship services, our ministries and each of our communities. Then, and only then, can we give the ministry back to the people – for those people will be empowered by the Spirit of God and then we will know what being the church really is.

Let me come at this from a different direction. For hundreds of years now the church has gathered every week around a sermon. The focal point of most church services is that sermon and we justify that because of our commitment to the Scriptures and the teaching of God's Word. Well, you may find it very interesting to know that Israel camped around the Presence of God. I don't believe that anything I could ever do or say in a sermon could impact you more than gathering in the actual presence of God. Since I embraced the call of God to full time ministry many decades ago, that has been my single greatest desire, my deepest longing and primary focus – to encourage, exhort, lead, guide and bring people into the presence of God Himself. That is the greatest gift I could ever give you. I recall a time recently when one of my congregation members said to me, *"You really do talk about God a lot, don't you?"* I smiled and said, "I certainly hope so – my most important task is to lead you to God."

Oh, that you would rend the heavens and come down.
(Isaiah 64:1)

That prayer has been prayed by revivalists for many centuries and historically we see times when the presence of God would be so strong, so pronounced in a preacher or evangelist, people would fall under conviction of sin and turn to God whenever they were just in the vicinity of that person!

One example I love to recount is that of the great American revival preacher Charles Finney in the late 1800's as he passed through the small community of Houghton in upstate New York. Finney was reading and praying on the train as the town flashed by his window, he was not even aware of it. But the Spirit of God was aware. As Charles Finney's train passed through that town, the Holy Spirit fell on people right across the community. Men in bars instantly fell to their knees under the conviction of the Holy Spirit and asked Jesus to save them. Churches across town were full the following Sunday as people came searching for God. Finney didn't even stop and never preached a sermon in the town of Houghton. It was the presence and power of God which accompanied Finney and his ministry which impacted that town. Now you might find that story a little fanciful but it happens to be true and whilst I believe in coincidences, I don't think what happened in the town of Houghton that day was anything other than a mighty move of God's Spirit.

"Oh, that you would rend the heavens and come down …" It's a great prayer, a powerful prayer, a legitimate prayer. But it's a prayer which has already been answered! In the first chapter of Mark's gospel, we read about the baptism of Jesus.' It says that

when Jesus came up out of the water, the heavens parted and the Holy Spirit came down upon Him in the form of a dove – and John's gospel adds the words, *"and remained."*

Jesus, and all present, were witnessing the answer to that prayer in Isaiah. When He saw the heavens parting, the word used for 'parting' there is the same word used in Matthew when he wrote about the temple veil being torn in two at the death of Jesus. It was a violent tearing of the veil and in that same verse it says the rocks around Jerusalem were torn apart – the same word – it is a violent rending, a tearing apart which cannot be put back together again. Those rocks would never be whole again. The temple veil would never be re-joined and the heavens would never be closed. That's right, the heavens will never again be closed. Isaiah's prayer has been answered.

As Jesus rose from the waters of baptism, there was a violent breaking of the powers of darkness which had clouded the minds of humanity for centuries. Now, here today, in Christ, the Holy Spirit rests upon and remains with every believer and our Father in heaven is jealous for fellowship with the Spirit that is within you and me and there is not a power in this universe which can get in the way of our Father's love.

You may have heard some modern preachers talk about 'closed heavens' which we need to 'open' by doing something, believing something or praying something. I cannot believe that such people read the same Bible as me! The only 'closed heavens' which exist are between the ears of believers as they fail to fully embrace the truth of who we are in Jesus Christ and Who resides within us: the Holy Spirit.

> *Greater is He that is in you than He that is in the world.*
> *(1 John 4:4)*

It is too easy for us to become fearful of darkness; fearful of the times we live in; fearful about the next news bulletin full of bad news about man's depravity and evil triumphing somewhere. It's too easy to focus on the accomplishments of darkness and doubt the accomplishments of God. We pray against darkness and against things which afflict us instead of learning how to respond to the voice and the actions of the Father, like Jesus did every day He was among us. If we live always in reaction to the darkness, then the devil is the one controlling our agenda and influencing what we do with our lives. But he doesn't have that right. He doesn't have the privilege to influence my agenda or yours at all. Jesus didn't live in reaction to the powers of darkness. He lived in response to the Father and said, *"I only do what I see My Father doing,"* and *"I only speak the words my Father gives me to speak."*

God is looking for a people who will embrace the privilege of living every day in response to God the Holy Spirit and a people who will not live one day in fear of the enemy or his accomplishments – because the gospel that is in your heart and mouth is more powerful than any dark force which has ever invaded this world. There is nothing that can stand in the way of the power of the resurrected Christ in us, through His Spirit.

Our God is looking for a people who will learn to be good stewards of all that He has given them; good stewards of the money and resources He bestows upon us; good stewards of the gifts and abilities He bestows upon us; good stewards of the freedom into which He has called us in Christ; but also good stewards of the Presence He has given us – the Holy Spirit. God wants to raise up a people who will usher in that Presence to every area of this dysfunctional world; people who are bold for Him; people who minister like Jesus did in the same power of the Holy Spirit like He did. But to be a good steward of the Presence of God in public, we must first be good stewards of His presence in private.

If you grew up in the church like me then you will remember the great stories about King David. The one I am drawn to most is the story about how this young man killed a lion and a bear with his own hands as he was watching over his father's sheep. What really impacts me about that story is David killed the lion and the bear when nobody was watching. That is what then qualified him to kill Goliath when two nations were watching. God is looking for a people who will win private victories in the secret places which are not for the audience or the applause of man. As we wrestle with our own doubts and fears; as our faith is formed in the crucible of life's trials; as we develop a personal history with God when nobody but Him is watching – then, and only then, are we ready for God to use us like He used Jesus. We have to believe that is possible. Jesus said, *"As I have been sent, so I am sending you."(John 20;21).* Jesus also said, *"Greater works than these shall you do."(John 14:12).* The more time we spend in the Gospels and the book of Acts, the more we will see and embrace Jesus, His mission, His passion, His purpose and His power.

Let me remind you of something which happened to Jesus one day when He walked among us. You can read about it in Luke chapter 8. Jesus was walking down the street one day and He was talking to people as He went. He was already well-known at this point. People had heard about His teaching and His miracles and so He couldn't really walk anywhere in public without drawing a crowd. As He walked along this day, He was teaching them and counselling them and praying for them as people were pressing in around Him – trying to get as close as they could so they could tell others, *"I saw Him."* or *"I was there when Jesus healed someone."* But in spite of this crowd which pressed in around him, somehow this one woman, who was not supposed to even be in public because of her physical condition, managed to push through as she reached out and touched a part of Jesus' clothing.

Now you have to picture this. Jesus is walking and talking and teaching and dialoguing with all these people. He is focused on multiple things, as well as not tripping and being trampled to death … when this one woman touches His clothing. She didn't touch Jesus – she only touched His garment. Immediately Jesus stopped and said, *"Power just left me – who did that?"* The power He is talking about is the person of the Holy Spirit.

So, just think about this. How conscious of the Holy Spirit's presence does someone need to be to realize in the midst of conversation, whilst walking with a crowd of people jammed in around them, to notice when somebody makes a withdrawal from their account? When I say withdrawal, I don't mean that Jesus lost some of the Holy Spirit or the presence of God. He was given the Spirit without measure – so He was not left without – but He did feel that presence flow into someone else. How aware of the Holy Spirit do you need to be to realize when someone has put a demand on that anointing?

It is one of the most fascinating stories about Jesus and worthy of our regular contemplation. At this point many modern Christians think, *'That's great, but I would expect that from Jesus – He was God.'* With that one dismissive, ignorant comment, we destroy the miracle of the incarnation and condemn ourselves and others to a life of mediocrity. Jesus did all His miracles as a man – not as God the Son. When Jesus took on human flesh, He took it on fully and completely and so He was born just like you and me with no special privilege or special powers because God the Son left all that in heaven when He chose to become a man. Anything and everything Jesus did, He chose to do the same way you and I will do – by the power and presence of the Holy Spirit within. That is why Jesus said, *"On my own I can do nothing."* We read that and ignore it's true meaning because we think the second person of the Trinity said those words. Well, He did, and that's where this gets a little complicated.

There is a line of teaching out there which says that Jesus 'could not' operate as God when He was in human form because Philippians 2:7 tells us that He left all of those 'powers' behind when he stepped out of heaven and into a teenager's womb. This miracle is what we call the incarnation and that's why we refer to Jesus as the 'incarnate Son of God.' It's a mystery; it's a true miracle; but it's not what some people say it is. Jesus did not 'give up' or 'lose' His power as the Son of God when we became one of us. He was still God, the Son. He could not stop being Who He was! I can't stop being who I am just by choosing to behave differently. I will always be who I am.

What Paul was saying in Philippians 2:7 was that Jesus, the incarnate Son of God, chose to operate within the confines of humanity so that we humans could relate to him and embrace His mission as humans. Theologically speaking, Jesus had to be fully human – just like us (there's another book in itself!). He also needed to be fully human so we could relate to Him and see what an authentic human being, fully surrendered to God, actually looks like and acts. Jesus' total dependence upon the Holy Spirit for every word, every miracle and every direction, every day of His earthly ministry was a deliberate choice. He needed us all to see and understand that He could do everything He did as a human being, just like us. Only then can we relate to Him; only then can we see that everything Jesus did as the incarnate Son of God, was a foretaste of what's to come when He commissions us.

Now by the end of Mark chapter 6 we see that the story of this woman being healed by touching Jesus' clothes spread like a fire. In today's lingo: it went viral.

> *And wherever he went - into villages, towns or countryside - they placed the sick in the marketplaces. They begged him to let them touch even the edge of his cloak, and all who touched it were healed. (Mark 6:56)*

All of this happened from the story of that one woman who did something nobody else had done before. But here's the crazy thing, Jesus never taught about touching anointed cloth to be healed. He never taught about this. But when we get into the book of Acts we see the Apostle Paul making tents and people would take his sweaty headbands and pieces of clothing from Paul and put them on demonized people and the demons would cry out and leave the person healed. Where did this come from? It came from the story of one woman touching the hem of Jesus' garment. But Paul never taught about this either. We have no evidence of him including this in any teaching he gave. Why? Well, we don't know, but personally, I just believe there are some things God won't let us find through instruction – He will only let us find them through experience.

But then Jesus' story and Paul's story are eclipsed by Peter's story. Also in the book of Acts we read where Peter would make a habit of going to prayer at a certain time of the day and they had discovered that when sick people just got close to Peter, they were healed. So, people began bringing their sick relatives and friends and have them lie beside where Peter walked so that as his shadow passed over them, they were healed. But you will not find an instruction manual or any teaching on the power of Holy Spirit anointed shadows. No such instruction existed. What does all this mean? It simply means this: God has made it possible for human beings to host His presence in such a way that we impact everything and everyone around us. This is an incarnational ministry if you want to call it that. This is where you and I must understand that we take the literal presence of Christ into every area of our lives.

When you stand in the queue at the supermarket or sit in the Doctor's waiting room - the presence of God, the manifestation of Christ is in that place and the more you believe that, the braver you will become in engaging people in conversation; you may even do something totally outrageous and ask them to join you for worship or at least have a cuppa and a chat.

The greatest news for every believer is that the Holy Spirit is in you. The same Holy Spirit Who was in Jesus when the woman touched His garment; the same Holy Spirit Who was in Paul throughout his four missionary journeys as people were healed by touching his sweat-soaked headband; the same Holy Spirit Who was so powerfully present in Peter that nobody had to even touch him or his clothing – they simply had to be near him! Do I really understand any of this? No. A lot of this wonderful life in Christ is a mystery which must be embraced by faith.

The Bible contains an enormous amount of instruction and teaching which we can know and embrace with our minds and our hearts. But the same Holy Spirit Who inspired what went into the Bible, also inspired what was left out. There are no detailed instructions about living and ministering in the power of the Holy Spirit. That's why they call this the Christian <u>faith</u>.

Often, we just don't understand, and yet we still believe, and when we believe, we receive. It's a faith journey from start to finish. Every sincere believer I have ever known is longing to find that 'peace which passes understanding,' but the only way to find a peace which passes understanding is to stop trying to understand it. This is true for us all but it's especially true for those in leadership in the church.

There will be times when God will ask us to travel a road which makes no sense and goes against what our minds tell us and yet, if we allow God's Spirit to minister to our spirit, we will realize that some of the most important decisions the people of God will make, do not come with the level of understanding we would like. In fact, some of them make no sense at all at the time. If you learn to be the resting place for the Holy Spirit Himself – then you will be amazed at what happens in and around you!

When the Holy Spirit rested upon and remained with Jesus after His baptism, it impacted how he lived every day. That's how Peter and Paul and all the early disciples lived. They were always conscious of the Spirit's presence and chose to be led by the Spirit, not by their own wisdom or the influence of others. That's why the ministry of Jesus was so powerful and so life changing. That's why His mission exploded across the world through His disciples over the next couple of hundred years.

Being the church will be nothing more than the title of a soon-forgotten book if we don't embrace what I have shared in this chapter particularly. My prayer is that those who have ears to hear, will really listen to what God is saying to the church right now. Are we even listening? More importantly, do we have the courage to respond?

CHAPTER THIRTEEN
Hearing from God

I think it is funny how so many scientists and medical experts are amazed at how well we human beings are designed and yet they don't believe in the Designer. The fact is, we humans have been wonderfully and intricately designed for many things, one of which is this: we are designed to hear from God. It's in our nature as born-again believers to have faith, but it's in our nature as human beings to hear from God. People will say, *'Well, I just don't hear God speak at all.'* If that is really true then those people may not be born again because our conversion is a response to God's personal invitation - it's never initiated by us. However, another reason why a person may think they do not hear from God is because they have a narrow view of how God speaks.

It's interesting how you can have an evangelistic gathering and preach the gospel and people will come to Christ. But very few of them would say, *'I clearly heard the voice of the Lord.'* They just listened to a preacher, they became aware of their need for God and they may even say they felt the presence of God. Well, all of that is actually the result of them hearing from God. The problem is we tend to put God on the same level as we humans talking to each other and yet God speaks in so many different ways. Sometimes He even speaks things that are so deep and so profound that He speaks directly to our spirit; He may deposit a thought or word that can take days, weeks or even months to unfold and enter our conscious mind.

There are times in our life when we might make a really good decision – one that bears incredible fruit for us or our family or our church. How did we get to that point? Well, there could be a number of reasons, but very often it was God's voice speaking into our situation and us not realizing that God had actually ministered to us in the night, weeks before the event because He knew what was coming and His presence in our life was His voice to our spirit. God prepared us for that decision.

On many occasions in my ministry, I have heard a brother or sister say something like, *"I'm in a very dry season right now; I'm just not hearing from the Lord very well. I can sense His presence at times but I can't hear His voice."*

Again, we reduce God to our human level. We know that a human being can be right in front of us but not say anything because their presence is not the same as their voice. But when God is present in Christ - He is the Word of God. When the Word shows up, so does His voice. We often don't interpret it as His voice and yet it is. Remember this truth:

If God is present, God is speaking, and God is always present.

So, there is a huge difference between God not speaking and us not hearing. The end result is the same – we don't hear from God – but the problem is always on our end. For example, at this very moment, regardless of where you are or what else you are doing, there are literally hundreds of voices bombarding you. There are at least ten television stations transmitting their signal; many more radio stations; hundreds of short-wave signals from right around the world are also occupying the same environment as you. There are police, fire and ambulance signals and who knows how many mobile phone transmissions are bouncing around you. They are all there, all the time. There's only one reason you cannot hear them – you are not tuned in.

Until you make a deliberate decision to tune in to those signals, you will never hear them. The same is true with God. He is always speaking collectively to the church and specifically to each of His children ... if only we had ears to hear.

In Luke chapter four, Jesus quotes a verse from the Old Testament, *"Man shall not live by bread alone, but by every word that proceeds from the mouth of God."* (Deuteronomy 8:3). We are alive, because God speaks. Our life is evidence of His voice. Even if it was possible for someone to not have the ability to hear from God, the moment God spoke, they would have that ability because God creates when He speaks. God spoke the whole world into being.

Faith comes by hearing, and hearing by the Word of God. (Romans 10:17)

Most of the sermons I have heard on the above verse conclude that faith comes from hearing the Word of God. That's not what it says. It says, faith comes from hearing. Hearing comes from the word of God. We listen to God's voice not to find something in addition to Scripture, but to clarify what has been inspired, written and preserved for us by the Holy Spirit.

You will recall that many years ago God spoke to Abraham and instructed him to sacrifice his son Isaac. But as the sword is coming down, the Lord spoke again and said, *"Never mind."* Now I am only speculating here, but I think Isaac was forever grateful that his dad kept listening to the Lord! Many 'Isaacs' have been slain because people listened to what God had said, but not to what God is saying now. It is the present tense voice of God which really builds our faith.

The very nature of faith implies I am hearing. You have a situation come up and you just believe God for a breakthrough and it comes because God speaks and you listen. You just may not have realised it was the voice of God before, but in time you will know. My hope and my prayer is that God will broaden our perception of how He speaks to us. I am sure that many of us have had unique experiences of the voice of the Lord, but what I would like to emphasize here is that you have been intentionally designed to perceive His voice. It's already in your design. In Hebrews 5:14 it talks about us having our senses trained to discern good and evil, having our human physical senses trained as we encounter the presence of God and the voice of God more and more.

You may already know this, but when they train people in banks to recognize counterfeit money, they only study the real money. They never study the counterfeit money. Day after day they immerse themselves in this study and become so exposed to the real thing that the counterfeit stands out. They may not even know at first why a note is counterfeit - they just know there's something wrong with it.

That's how you discern good and evil. You don't discern evil by studying evil; you become so immersed in the Person of God that anything that doesn't fit with God's goodness becomes very obvious. So, we need to understand now that in essence, God's presence is God's voice. That doesn't mean we go looking for His voice every time we are in His presence. His presence is an end in itself. God longs for us to hang out with Him and enjoy that intimacy the Holy Spirit can bring in worship times, prayer times or when meditating on the Scriptures. Don't be quick to try to figure out what God's doing. Just be a pliable, teachable, hungry and thirsty child. Just be the sailboat with a sail that is set and ready to be moved by the wind of the Spirit, regardless of the direction it takes you. Don't try to work out what the wind is doing – just submit to it.

Perhaps I could put this another way: we'll never discover God through analysis. We only discover God through surrender. It's not that understanding is wrong - God tells us in the Bible to pursue wisdom and understanding - it's vital. But the problem occurs when we only obey and embrace what we understand. Because then we have a God who looks a lot like us, we reduce Him to our size so He is more easily comprehended. God is looking for a people who are yielded to Him and who say 'Yes' before He even speaks and it's that 'yes' before He speaks that will always attract His voice.

I remember hearing a story a years ago of a Christian family who were driving on a mountain road when their little boy, just out of nowhere, declares, *"There's a big rock on the road right around the next bend."* His father was driving and was somewhat stunned by the words his son just spoke out of the blue and so he immediately slowed down as he approached the bend. Just as he got past the main curve, there it was, this huge rock in the middle of the road. Dad was so impressed that his boy had heard from God he said, *"So what else is God saying son?"* Without missing a beat, the young boy replied, *"God said we need to stop at McDonalds when we get to town."* We can laugh at the young boy but that is so like us, isn't it? We get it right once … let's see if we can extend it into our will.

Hearing from God is a moment-by-moment thing. We don't get to determine when He speaks or what He says, but we should not expect it to come the same way or via the same means. Of one thing we can be certain though: God is always speaking. In fact, it says in Hebrews 1:3 it that God sustains or upholds all things by the power of His Word. Think about that. The billions of universes out there are actually held in place because God speaks. You have the capacity to read this book because God speaks. It is God's voice that keeps you alive; keeps you engaged. So much of what we understand in life came simply because God spoke to us through the Scriptures; or in our sleep; or He spoke to us through a friend; a circumstance; a situation; He arranged all the players in our life to deliver an insight at a particular time, in preparation for a decision we make that may radically change the course of our whole life.

God is always speaking into our lives; always building into us the ability to become the Word made flesh. Forgive me if that sounds blasphemous, let me explain. Jesus Christ is the Word made flesh – that's true. But it's also true that we are in Christ. Jesus is always wanting His Word to be made flesh, again and again, which is why He wants people like you and me to model and illustrate exactly what He says so that when people look at our lives, they see the life of Christ; they see what has been written in Scripture. For us to live like that, we must first believe that God is always speaking and second, we must be living in continuous anticipation of what God might be saying and doing in us, around us and through us.

Of course, there are times when God's word is so clear, He may as well be shouting. But then there are many times when God speaks very softly and that's when we need to focus very carefully. Some people call it 'leaning in.' You know that when you are listening to a softly spoken person and you really want to hear what they are saying because it's important to you .. you literally lean in so you can hear better. Or you might be standing in a line waiting to be served and you hear a conversation close by which sounds fascinating and before you know it, you find yourself leaning in so you can hear clearly.

That's the image I get when I think of a child of God who is committed to hearing every word from God. The whole point is this: when we want to hear, we lean in, we anticipate the Lord speaking to us and we have the willingness to obey before He even speaks. When God encounters that intentional listening and that willingness to say 'yes' before He speaks – He is delighted and will say more than you ever imagined.

Hearing from God can be a struggle for many believers and it shouldn't be. It's your nature to hear from God. It's how He made you. It's who you are. It's in your design. Everything about you was wired and designed to perceive, to recognize, to hear and to have fellowship with God. I'm not as good at hearing God as I would like to be, but I'm certainly better at it than I used to be. That's all God expects - a gradual journey of discovery as we learn to discern His voice. But it's your 'yes' before He speaks which positions you to hear Him better.

Whenever anyone turns to the Lord, the veil is taken away. (2 Corinthians 3:16)

Some think that is a strange verse. You would think that the veil is taken away so the person could turn to the Lord. But in His mercy, the veil isn't lifted until they turn, because there's enough evidence of the voice of God for every human being. We are without excuse. Paul made it very clear here:

For since the creation of the world God's invisible qualities - His eternal power and divine nature - have been clearly seen, being understood from what has been made, so that people are without excuse. (Romans 1:20)

So, we are all created in the image of God and God's nature is revealed in so many ways throughout His creation. But when His people, who are called by His name, decide to intentionally turn to the Lord and 'lean in' to hear His voice – God removes the veil completely. Whatever kept us from our clear perception of the things of God is lifted and we can hear and see clearly. But what regulates that clarity is our 'yes' before He speaks and our deep, ongoing commitment to hear from God.

Now it goes without saying, but perhaps the most important pre-requisite to hearing from God is our desire to do so. I know that sounds dumb but believe me when I tell you that there are millions of prayers rising to heaven right now across the earth from people who really don't want to hear from God. If you could listen carefully to the words they are praying, they are really telling God what He needs to do and presenting Him with a list of tasks to complete which we are not able to do ourselves. That's not hearing from God.

We read in Psalm 40:8 where King David cried out to God and said, *"My God, I want to do what you want."* No shopping list here. No instructions for God. Just a soft, teachable, willing heart and a loud 'yes' before God even speaks. A lot of people talk to God but rarely hear from God. For them, prayer is a monologue. But you can't have a real relationship through a monologue. A real relationship requires a dialogue – where both parties speak and both parties hear. You've got to really want to hear from God more than anything else. It is at that point when promises like these become your own:

> *… if you seek the Lord your God, you will find him if you seek him with all your heart and with all your soul.*
> *(Deuteronomy 4:29)*

> *"For I know the plans I have for you," declares the Lord, "plans to prosper you and not to harm you, plans to give you hope and a future. Then you will call on me and come and pray to me, and I will listen to you. You will seek me and find me when you seek me with all your heart. I will be found by you," declares the Lord.*
> *(Jeremiah 29:11-14a)*

> *"Be still and know that I am God." (Psalm 46:10)*

That last verse is the key. We live in a fast paced, crowded, world. We're surrounded by so many sounds, signals and lots of competing voices every day. Being still, so we might discern the presence and voice of God, has never been harder than it is today and it has never been more important that we hear from God.

Let me finish this important chapter with a story which I hope will remain with you. Before refrigerators, people in the north of Canada used icehouses to preserve their food. Icehouses had thick walls, no windows and a tightly fitted door. In winter, when streams and lakes were frozen, large blocks of ice were cut, hauled to the icehouses and covered with sawdust. Often the ice would last well into the summer. One day this man lost his very valuable watch while he was out working in his icehouse. He searched diligently for it, carefully raking through the sawdust, but he didn't find it. His fellow workers also looked, but their efforts also proved futile. A small boy who heard about the fruitless searches, quietly slipped into the icehouse during the noon hour and soon emerged with the watch. Amazed, the men asked him how he found it. The boy explained:

"I found the watch the only way I could. I closed the door, lay down in the sawdust, and kept very, very still, focussing only on the watch and listened very, very carefully. It wasn't long before I could hear the watch ticking and then I knew exactly where it was."

That simple story has never left me and every time I read or hear Psalm 46:10, *"Be still and know that I am God,"* the Holy Spirit reminds me of that young boy and his simple, yet profound explanation of how we can hear from God.

CHAPTER FOURTEEN
Abiding in Christ

Let me review where we've come thus far in this study of what being the church means. We began by examining our roots and looking at how well equipped the church was in those first 200-300 years after Christ was here in the flesh. We also saw what went wrong and how quickly a dynamic, integrated network of Spirit-led house churches, growing rapidly in spite of the severe persecution, became a State-sanctioned religious organisation with large, centralised meeting places and a rapidly diminishing number of ministers of the gospel. Then we were confronted and encouraged by the promise of God from long ago:

> *If my people who are called by my name will humble themselves and pray and seek my face and turn from their sin, then I will hear from heaven, forgive their sin and heal their land.*
> *(2 Chronicles 7:14)*

That is a promise God has never withdrawn and it may well be more important today than when those words were first spoken. We live in a time when the nations of the world are desperate for a mighty move of God and the spotlight is turned on the church; the people of God; the custodians of the gospel of God's amazing grace; the ones who hold the keys to heaven and the answers to all the problems in our world today.

This is why we need to know what being the church really is as the church becomes the army of God once again. However, as we saw in chapter three, the greatest enemy we face every day is what I suggested is the mother and father of all sins and the greatest single barrier to that community-wide transformation we long for; that enemy is unbelief. Using the image of the parable of the Sower, we were reminded about the many weeds of unbelief which grow in the garden of our heart and how important it is for us to be diligent in tending that garden so that once again we believe what God has said and walk into the reality of all His great promises to those who believe.

In the previous chapter, I affirmed that humans are designed to hear from God, that God speaks to us in a myriad of ways and for us to live and move and have our being in Christ; for us to fulfil His mission on earth; for us to be fully equipped as the church; then like Jesus, when He walked among us as a man, we need to learn how to hear from God.

As a man, Jesus said that He only did what He saw the Father doing and only spoke the words the Father gave Him to speak (See John 5). For that to happen, Jesus developed the ability as a man to hear from God and be guided by the Holy Spirit. He then modelled that close, personal, intimate relationship with God into which each and every one of us has been called. So, I want to continue that thought as we look at perhaps the best chapter in the whole Bible which explains what that abiding relationship with God in Christ looks like.

Chapter 15 of John's Gospel is well known for two primary reasons. Firstly, this is where Jesus says to His disciples, *"No longer do I call you servants ... but I have called you friends."* (v.15) This is also the chapter where Jesus gives us that very powerful illustration of the nature of a believer in relationship with God. He uses four key components in this metaphor: the vine, the branches, the vine dresser and the fruit. The vine dresser (gardener), the one who owns the vineyard, is our Heavenly Father. Jesus Himself is the vine. The people of God (you and me) are the branches and the fruit is that which is naturally produced because of our connection to Jesus, the vine.

I want you to notice I said it is *naturally produced*. No fruit tree, no vegetable garden, no vineyard has to groan and travail or struggle and strain to bring forth fruit. It bears fruit naturally, provided it is well-fed, well-watered and pruned correctly. Yes, pruning is vitally important. God rewards all growth with pruning. Pruning in the Kingdom of heaven is not punishment. People look at the discipline of God and they often assume that the discipline or the pruning of the Lord is punishment. That's not true as we will see in a moment. Let's look at the first eight verses of John chapter fifteen. Jesus is speaking here:

> *I am the true vine, and my Father is the gardener. He cuts off every branch in me that bears no fruit, while every branch that does bear fruit he prunes[a] so that it will be even more fruitful. You are already clean because of the word I have spoken to you. Remain in me, as I also remain in you. No branch can bear fruit by itself; it must remain in the vine. Neither can you bear fruit unless you remain in me.*
>
> *I am the vine; you are the branches. If you remain in me and I in you, you will bear much fruit; apart from me you can do nothing. If you do not remain in me, you are like a branch that is thrown away and withers; such branches are picked up, thrown into the fire and burned. If you remain in me and my words remain in you, ask whatever you wish, and it will be done for you. This is to my Father's glory, that you bear much fruit, showing yourselves to be my disciples. (John 15:1-8)*

Do you remember the parable of Jesus about the landowner who gave each of his ten servants a sum of money? Or perhaps the parable of the talents where three people are given some money with the hope that they would invest their talent wisely and bring a return to the landowner? From the very beginning, God created everything to be productive. Every living thing is meant to bear fruit. By nature, everything about our life is designed to be productive and fruit-bearing.

God is glorified by the system He created, where a peach tree will grow peaches, you eat the fruit, you plant the seed, and it grows another tree that brings forth more peaches. That cycle of life and productivity is a cycle God created. God's economy is linked directly to His voice, which is not only all-powerful, it is also creative in nature. God spoke and said, *"Let there be light"* and there was light. So, as we saw in the previous chapter, God's design is that everything would happen through the power of His Word.

In John 16, the very next chapter, Jesus describes how He has re-inherited everything as a man. The Father has effectively given everything back into His hands. As we know, Jesus chooses to not assert His divinity when He becomes a man. He is still entirely God, but He chooses to set aside His deity to take on flesh and live with all the reality and restrictions of a human being, although He is still eternally God. So, in that position, as a man, He now re-inherits everything He already possessed as God. He inherits everything as a man and because we now stand in Christ, He includes us in His inheritance.

All that belongs to the Father is mine. That is why I said the Spirit will receive from me what he will make known to you. (John 16:15).

Jesus is not merely making an announcement here; He's not just showing off what He owns; He is transferring resources from a heavenly account into an earthly account and that transfer takes place whenever He speaks. Not only does God create; not only does He transfer resources through His decree, but the Bible says (Hebrews 1:3) that every molecule is held in place, by the power of His word. Everything is defined, everything is empowered, everything is created, everything is sustained through His Word.

Therefore, when we come to John 15 and this illustration of us being the branches of a vine, we have the Father God as the vine dresser and Jesus as the vine. He said that every branch in Him that does not bear fruit, He takes away and every branch that bears fruit, He prunes, so that it may bear more fruit. He rewards all of our growth with pruning. In verse 3 Jesus said, *"You are already clean because of the word I've spoken to you."* So, he's saying that when we bear fruit, He will have to prune us over and over again because that way, we'll bear even more fruit.

The Lord does everything for the purpose of increase. He thinks in terms of things working, to better our life, to bring increase; to be productive. The sun gives light and heat; the leaves of the trees give oxygen; plants give seed to reproduce. God has created a cycle of increase and productivity. He has brought you and me into that life cycle with supernatural increase and supernatural supply. He has positioned us to bring increase, but not an increase that we have to create. It's the increase that comes automatically by remaining attached to the vine. It's normal. It's guaranteed. It's part of His master design.

He'll do the pruning; we just need to stay firmly attached. We don't have to make ourselves grow - we just have to stay connected to or 'abide' in the vine. So, Jesus said, *"You are already clean because of the word I've spoken to you."*

It's important we know that the Greek word translated here as *clean* is essentially the same word as the one translated *prune*. When Jesus says His disciples are clean already, He is saying, *"I've already pruned you."* How did He prune them? By the word He has spoken. The pruning wasn't with a hand it was with His voice and it wasn't yelling and screaming, it was just Jesus speaking the truth, adjusting values, expectations and priorities so they could be more fruitful. He was always pruning their value system and their interpretation of things.

For example, in Luke 9 Jesus sends the disciples out on a ministry trip and they are very, very productive. They come back with stories of breakthroughs: they saw miracles happen they had never seen except for Jesus, but now they actually saw it happen through their hands, through their words and they're beside themselves with excitement. They are very enthusiastic when they return.

The very next moment you find them chatting in a group without Jesus there, and when Jesus turns up, He asks them what they are talking about. Of course, He already knows what they were talking about - they are arguing about who is the greatest among them. It is interesting how some things that are in your heart will not be revealed by failure and weakness, they will only be revealed through success.

We know that the hardest place to minister is at home and so Jesus sent them home to minister. Because a prophet is not without honour, except in his hometown, so if you can minister at home, you'll learn to do ministry out of obedience instead of for applause. When Jesus sends them home, breakthroughs happen and they bring the reports back. But in the very next scene, because of their success, they are arguing about who is the greatest. It wasn't failure in ministry that caused this problem - it was the fact that they were fruitful; they had stuff happen and they didn't think it happened to any other disciple.

So, Jesus talks to them about what greatness really is. Jesus needed to do some pruning and He did it with His words. You see, people who hang out with Jesus begin to dream of personal significance in ways they never dreamed of before. There is something special about being with people that believe in you. Jesus trusted them and believed in them enough to turn them loose on their own cities. Having somebody believe in them stirred something up that was powerful and right. It was a sense of personal significance and they bore rich fruit; they saw the miracles; they had healings and deliverance; people believed the gospel. That's good fruit but when they came back together, they argued about who was the greatest - that's not good fruit.

I want you to picture this branch of the vine and this huge bunch of grapes that has formed, that's the good fruit. But then the branch keeps growing and growing with only leaves and no fruit. It's a great looking branch and the leaves are awesome but God wants them to be productive. So, He rewards their growth with pruning. He points to what is developing in them, which is not healthy, doesn't make sense and brings them glory outside the Lordship of Jesus and He cuts it off. So now that branch can re-shoot at that point and produce real fruit. By the power of His word, Jesus pruned a branch in His vine.

Take Peter, for example. His boldness is great to a point, but past that point he has foot-in-mouth disease all the time; talking at the wrong time; interrupting God; rebuking Jesus when He talked about His impending death and telling Him that going to the cross is a bad idea. However, with that same boldness, when Peter is submitting to the Lordship of Jesus, we see him standing before a crowd of thousands who were mocking the outpouring of the Spirit and he preaches a sermon that brings thousands into the Kingdom of Heaven. That boldness outside of the Lordship of Jesus caused him problems - that boldness under the Lordship of Jesus brought tremendous fruit.

So, when God sees a branch that's grown way past its ability to bear fruit, He cuts it back. The pain of that pruning can be significant, but the pruning is what actually brings more fruit. In the very next scene, the disciples are talking to Jesus and they said, *"We saw this group over here, and they were trying to cast demons in your name. We told them to stop."* By inference, they were saying, *"They aren't part of the inner crowd. We are Jesus' disciples and only we get to do that."* Now their loyalty to the group was healthy. In a sense, it was right. It was good. But loyalty to one in the kingdom never requires disloyalty to another. That's carnal and natural loyalty which is humanistic loyalty. That is not kingdom loyalty. So, when they said, *"We told them to stop,"* Jesus got out His pruning shears and said, *"No, guys, listen, if they're not against us, they're for us."* Well, that was the whole new concept.

Once again, we have a branch that is bearing fruit but then it grows beyond the point of fruit-bearing and so God prunes it back, to ensure more fruit later. He didn't lower them. He didn't belittle them. He didn't punish them. He instead spoke to the issue and as long as we are hearers of the Word, as long as we are willing for God to speak change into our life, pruning will always bring forth fruit in time.

> *I am the vine; you are the branches. If you remain in me and I in you, you will bear much fruit; apart from me you can do nothing (John 15:5)*

So, Jesus announces here that we can do nothing without Him. But ten chapters earlier He announced that He can do nothing without the Father. So, can you see that He's trying to bring us into the same place of dependency that He lives in? He has set the example; He has modelled the lifestyle and the value system; from day one He's working to bring us into the same place of dependency. He could do nothing without the Father. That's how much He emptied himself. He's still eternally God but He emptied Himself, He set to one side His deity, so He could function as a human being who was completely dependent on the Father throughout His whole ministry. In so doing He set a powerful example for us and effectively puts us in a position where we can do nothing of any significance in His Kingdom apart from Him. Which means we're going to have to learn dependency to pull this off because He is expecting fruitfulness.

Therefore, what is our responsibility? Abide in Christ; stay connected to the vine. We don't focus on fruit bearing – we focus on abiding and staying connected to the vine. The fruit is the natural outcome of abiding. That's why we need to hear from God every day. We need to really listen and allow the corrective Word of the Lord to prune us when needed and the fruit will come naturally by virtue of our abiding in the vine. As we listen to what He says, the fruit will always form. But we must stay connected to the vine. When a branch is not connected, it's just a useless stick.

> *If you remain in me and my words remain in you, ask whatever you wish, and it will be done for you. (John 15:7)*

God is glorified through fruit and in this particular verse, the fruit is answered prayer. But just make sure you understand the context here. He's not answering any whim because He refuses to answer any prayer that undermines His purpose and our purpose in Christ. What's supposed to happen in our walk with the Lord is that desires are formed in us as the offspring of our walk with God. Dreams and desires form because of our time spent abiding in Christ. We don't just come in prayer with our shopping list - our prayers emerge from the depth of our abiding, our sharing in the heart of God.

That's the context of being called friends. Why did Jesus say, *"I no longer call you servants, I call your friends."* Because the servant doesn't know what the master is doing. The servant doesn't get a picture of what's happening behind the scenes where God shares His heart and says, *"This is what moves me, this is what marks me, this is my value system."* The servant doesn't get access to that. But the friend does. As friends we get to see what moves the heart of God and then we pray accordingly. We pray out of an understanding of His heart. We pray out of this position of great privilege.

The word translated here as *'anything you desire'* is tied to the will of God. In New Testament Greek there are two words for the will of God. One is that which is concrete, it's established. You can vote yes or no, it doesn't matter – it is going to happen anyway. It's like saying you don't believe Jesus is coming back. Well, that doesn't matter, it's happening and you don't get to vote. Your prayer has nothing to do with it. Your belief system has nothing to do with it. He's just decided He's going to do it, so it is going to be done. That's one aspect of the will of God. But there's another part of the will of God which can be described as a dream or desire or wish of God. He can do anything He wants, but His dream is not the outcome. His dream is the journey with yielded people that help bring about the desired outcome. He values the journey above the destination. He willingly submits His sovereignty to the actions of His much-loved children.

So then, in practical terms, we play a vital part in His will being done. He brings us into this special relationship where we have the privilege of discerning His heart, His dreams, His desires, His ultimate will and we then make that the cry of our heart. It's a prayer where we say, *"God, we want your dreams and desires to unfold here as they do in heaven."* It's a mirroring of the heart of God. By abiding in Him, we learn His heart and can begin to mirror it back to Him, not as robots but as sons and daughters who learn what our destiny is all about so that the cries of our heart are a reflection of the cries of God's heart.

There's something happening in that merging of hearts, that marriage of hearts, where the Father becomes glorified, because He delights in our cry. So can you see how God created a system whereby a covenant people can make a difference in the course of world history, a covenant people can have prayers answered, and it is God's delight to do so.

> *You did not choose me, but I chose you and appointed you so that you might go and bear fruit - fruit that will last - and so that whatever you ask in my name the Father will give you.*
> *(John 15:16)*

Jesus is making the relational connection between a yielded heart and a generous heart so that His purposes will be fully realized in the earth and all creation will celebrate His plan. The world will notice. His plan really worked: broken, destroyed, hell-bent humanity is redeemed and now they're making a difference in the course of world history. We never thought it could work, but it's working. Look, they are forgiven and now they look so much like Jesus. This is amazing. It's working. All of creation groans and travails for the sons and daughters of God to realize who they are and take their rightful place.

Heaven is waiting to celebrate the answers to our prayers. But not just the result of a request ... but the result of us saying 'yes' to a journey ... saying 'yes' to abiding in the vine, Jesus. Hear the Word of the Lord again today:

> *I am the vine; you are the branches. If you remain in me and I in you, you will bear much fruit; apart from me you can do nothing. (John 15:5)*

Apart from the Vine, you can do nothing. Abide in the vine and you can do anything and everything God desires and the world will finally see the Glory of God across the earth, in and through His surrendered, abiding sons and daughters. The world will finally see the church in all her glory, as God always intended. Now if your heart is not pounding in your chest right now - then please check you have a pulse!

CHAPTER FIFTEEN
Walking in the Spirit

The Holy Spirit played a very important role in the life of Jesus of Nazareth and in the life of the early church He birthed, the church which Jesus is still building today through His Spirit. As a flesh and blood human being, Jesus learned how to 'host' the Holy Spirit and defer to Him at every point in His journey. Then before He left the earth, He told His disciples to wait until the Holy Spirit came so that they could do the same.

As disciples of Jesus here and now, we are also called to live in step with the Holy Spirit every moment of every day. We have more than a message to deliver; we have more than a job, an occupation or a ministry to steward; we have a Person – a Person Who has so intimately and so intensely devoted Himself to us, He rests upon us and is released within us - literally changing our environment wherever we go.

The Holy Spirit has been given to us without measure and without limit. Any limitations are on our side of this glorious partnership. We are the ones who deny ourselves, our families, the church and our nation the power and wonder of *'Christ in us, the hope of glory.'* We are the ones who grieve and quench the Holy Spirit and deny Him access to our thoughts, our hearts, our lives and our wills. This whole concept of God the Holy Spirit resting on us and flowing through us is awesome, it's extreme, it's mind-boggling – but it also happens to be true.

Jesus made a very interesting statement one day when He was here among us. We can read it in John 6:63. He said, *"The words that I speak to you are spirit, and they are life." (NASB)* Think through this. This particular sermon of Jesus was probably the most offensive He gave in His entire ministry. He started with a crowd of almost twenty thousand people and He ended up with just a handful of disciples. He offended the crowd so much that most of them walked away and refused to accept anything He was teaching.

Jesus was simply telling them what the Father told Him to say, through the Spirit. Sometimes God will bring a word to us that we don't understand or accept, just to test our heart. Did you know that God is in the business of revealing hearts? Well, He very often does that by offending our minds. At such times we are forced to ask,

> *'Am I in this for intellectual gratification? Do I need to be in control? Do I need to manage this issue or these people? ... or ... am I totally yielded and surrendered in my relationship with God and am I willing to embrace what I don't understand?'*

That's what submitting to the Lordship of Christ looks like in our lives. It's when we are truly able to say, *'I don't get this; I don't understand this; but I do know His voice and I will heed that voice.'* When we step outside human reasoning and our own sense of personal control, then all of heaven shows up to confirm and celebrate our obedience to the Lord.

Every believer is put into such a position many times in their lives and some of us let our flesh, our mind, our pride, our fallen humanity have their way and some of us let the Spirit of God have His way. The outcome of that choice is very significant. One feeds and empowers our flesh and our need to control people and the circumstances of life - the other empowers our surrender to the Holy Spirit and Christ's mission to advance His kingdom.

Let me tell you, from personal experience, from counselling and from walking alongside thousands of brothers and sisters over many years, that you will not experience the peace of God which passes all understanding until you give up the need to understand! There are many things I understand about God, my life and the mission of Christ. For that I am grateful. But that understanding is a bonus, it's not my right and nor do I have to understand in order to follow God's voice.

One of the most powerful and liberating things a human being can do before God is to lay down the right to be in control and choose to follow the Spirit – even if, and especially when, we don't fully understand what's happening or why.

There are two important instructions the Apostle Paul gives us regarding this relationship with the Holy Spirit and they are both essential. The first one is in Ephesians 4:30, *"Do not grieve the Holy Spirit."* The second one is in 1 Thessalonians 5:19, *"Do not quench the Holy Spirit."* These two warnings serve as guard rails, if you like, in our walk with God. As we journey through life and are careful not to grieve or quench the Holy Spirit in thought, word or deed, then our relationship with Him and our understanding of His role in our life and the ministry of the church continues to grow and mature and God's empowering presence grows accordingly. I'll come back to those two guard rails later but let me go back to what Jesus said.

"The words that I speak to you are spirit, and they are life." Jesus is the Word made flesh, and when He speaks, the Word of God is made Spirit. Something happens when you find the heartbeat of God and speak it out. You may know this from experience. Many of us in ministry have been in that situation when we are talking with a brother or sister about God and it might be in a home group or just over coffee and we are discussing the things of God and then out of our own mouth comes words which are so spot on, so appropriate, so right for that moment, that there is no way in the world that we thought that stuff up! Suddenly the whole atmosphere changes and there is a Presence which we did not experience before. What just happened? It's simple really. God gave us words which became Spirit and that Spirit gave life!

We are responsible stewards of the words of a Person and each day we travel between these guard rails of grieving the Spirit or quenching the Spirit and as we learn how to move in that anointed space, our lives and ministries are transformed. These are not legalistic barriers; they are necessary guard rails which we should welcome.

To grieve the Spirit is to sin in thought, in ambition or in attitude of heart. That grieves Him and brings Him much pain when we choose to do something that would undermine our purpose and our calling in Christ. To quench the Spirit means we restrict the flow of the Spirit. We hinder His movement in us or those around us or in our ministry or the church.

You know how you pick up a garden hose which is running, usually with a sprinkler on the end, and you kink the hose to stop the flow so you can move the sprinkler? Well, that's the concept behind this word *quench*. We can restrict the flow of the Spirit through our unbelief or our need to control people or situations or through our demonic fears and doubts. Grieving is about character. Quenching is about power and flow. Which is more important – character or power? Well, that's like asking which wing on a bird is more important, the left or the right? Obviously, both are essential and equally important.

Jesus is calling a people to Himself who can display purity and power and this relationship we have with the Holy Spirit puts us in that place where deep in our heart of hearts we have the confidence that nothing is impossible with God. God wants to raise up a people who will no longer be satisfied with human accomplishments which we then call ministry. I am thankful for the talents, skills and experience which people in the church have been given. I am thankful for the buildings we can erect and enjoy in the Lord's name. I am thankful for the works of service we can perform and the mission projects we can launch or support. That's all great, but at the end of the day if we have not truly invaded the impossible, the supernatural, then we have not demonstrated the gospel as it was meant to be demonstrated.

The things that you and I should remember most are the things that we cannot take any credit for – the things that we saw God and God alone do. How did Jesus turn the world on its head, impact so many people and draw such huge crowds? It's simple, when people came to Jesus they encountered God, through the power of the Holy Spirit. Why did the early church then explode across the world and unite the most divided human community in history, reaping such a mighty harvest for so long? It was because when people came into contact with the early Apostles and disciples, they encountered God through the supernatural work of the Holy Spirit.

When Jesus Himself said, *"On my own I can do nothing,"* that is exactly what He meant. Without the presence, power and ministry of the Holy Spirit in Jesus and through Jesus, all the world had was a carpenter from Nazareth with a few radical ideas! Without the presence and power of the Holy Spirit, that special day of Pentecost would never have happened; the church would never have been born; and history would never have been re-written by a handful of ordinary people. Without the presence and power of the Holy Spirit right here and now, in your life, in my life, in the church and in its leaders, we have nothing to give, nothing to say and nothing we could possibly do which would impact the world around us!

To those who may long to see their church building full to overflowing one day I say this: God is not going to send people to us so they can encounter the pastor or the musicians or the singers. God will send people to us when He knows those people will encounter their God in our midst and when they do, they will never be the same again - and nor will the church. Our programs, our ministries, our services, our sermons, our songs, our prayers, our very lives mean nothing, will amount to nothing and will have zero impact on the needs of this world, until we learn to walk in the Spirit as Jesus walked in the Spirit.

Without the active ministry of the Spirit of God we have nothing to give, nothing to offer and no power to change anything in this dysfunctional, broken world! God is the only One Who has ever changed history and God will change history again through us, here and now, if we let the Holy Spirit have His way in us and among us! The power of the gospel needs to flow through yielded vessels who say, *'I'm tired of the status quo; I'm tired of routine; I'm tired of traditional boundaries; I want to see Jesus glorified the way He is in the Book!* When Jesus sent his disciples out, His instructions were as simple as they were confronting:

> *As you go, proclaim this message: 'The kingdom of heaven has come near.' Heal the sick, raise the dead, cleanse those who have leprosy, drive out demons. Freely you have received; freely give. (Matthew 10:7-8)*

Jesus gave them a sermon to preach: *'The kingdom of heaven is at hand.'* That is probably the shortest sermon in history, because

Jesus didn't want them to just preach. He wanted them to see the fruit of that short sermon. Saying the kingdom of heaven is at hand without demonstrating that reality, would be a waste of time. Jesus wanted the disciples to demonstrate the reality of the kingdom, by healing the sick, cleansing the lepers, raising the dead and casting out demons!

Now there are a lot of people in the church today who don't know what to do with those two verses from Matthew 10. Many people just ignore them. Some fear them and wish they were not there. Some just don't believe them and others are challenged by them. But these verses are like 'Ministry 101' for the disciples of Jesus. Just picture it. Jesus pulls them together and they sit in a circle, and He says something like this:

> *Ok team, it's time for you to do the stuff. It's time for you to embrace your calling, pursue your purpose and truly follow Me. Here is what you need to preach. Write this down. 'The Kingdom of heaven is at hand.' That's it. Then, you need to show them what the kingdom of heaven looks like. You need to release heaven on earth as you heal the sick, cleanse the lepers, raise the dead and cast out demons. I have already given you everything you need freely, so now get out there and freely give it away.*

Then down in verse 12 Jesus says, "As you enter the home, give it your greeting. If the home is deserving, let your peace rest on it .." Just hold that thought for a moment as we go way back to Noah:

> *"He (Noah) sent out a dove to see if the water had receded from the surface of the ground. But the dove could find nowhere to perch because there was water over all the surface of the earth; so it returned to Noah in the ark. He reached out his hand and took the dove and brought it back to himself in the ark. He waited seven more days and again sent out the dove from the ark.*
>
> *When the dove returned to him in the evening, there in its beak was a freshly plucked olive leaf! Then Noah knew that the water had receded from the earth. He waited seven more days and sent the dove out again, but this time it did not return to him. (Genesis 8:8-12)*

What is the international sign of peace? A dove with an olive branch in its mouth, right? Fascinating. In what form did the Holy Spirit descend and rest upon Jesus at His baptism? A dove, right? So, the Old Testament story of Noah and the dove is a prophetic picture of New Testament, new covenant ministry.

Jesus said we are to go into a house and release peace there. Luke's gospel says that if there's nobody in that house worthy to receive that peace, then that dove, that peace will return to you like it did to Noah all those years ago. If you remember nothing else from this chapter, remember this: You and I are ministers of a Person. We have more than words, more than a message, more than a concept, more than a spiritual argument to give to people. We have a Person resting upon us and residing within us Who longs to be released into the environment in which God has placed us.

What was it that was drawn from Jesus when the woman touched His garment and He felt power move from Him? What was it that was drawn from Jesus in town after town over those three and half years of intense ministry? It was the person of the Holy Spirit – given to us without measure, without limitation to impart to any and all who receive Him. That is the normal Christian life! That is why we are here: to advance the kingdom of heaven, by God's grace, for God's glory and through God's Spirit. That is being the church! Now let's take a look at something which happened after the resurrection of Jesus:

> *On the evening of that first day of the week, when the disciples were together, with the doors locked for fear of the Jewish leaders, Jesus came and stood among them and said, "Peace be with you!" (John 20:19)*

Remember what Jesus taught them to do when they entered a house? *'Let your peace come upon it.'* Well, this is where I think they finally understood what He was talking about.

> *After he said this, he showed them his hands and side. The disciples were overjoyed when they saw the Lord. Again Jesus said, "Peace be with you!"*

> *"As the Father has sent me, I am sending you." And with that he breathed on them and said, "Receive the Holy Spirit."*
> *(John 20:19-22)*

What happened here? Jesus walked into a room full of fearful believers and released the peace of another world in the Person of the Holy Spirit. You and I are called to walk into a world full of fearful people and bring that peace. We need a generation of people who can walk into a room, into a community, into a city and a nation and bring the hope, healing and reality of another world through the person of the Holy Spirit. Jesus walked into that room and said "Peace" and they didn't receive it at first because they were fearful – and understandably - some guy who was dead just walked through a closed door! So, Jesus said it again and His words became Spirit and He imparted a Person to them, not a hollow platitude or a powerless blessing.

Is any of this making sense to you? I pray that it is because all ministry involves us learning to cooperate with the Holy Spirit and then to impart Him to others. Do you remember in Noah's story that the dove flew around looking for a place to land? Do you understand that the Holy Spirit is always looking for a resting place in another person? He is always looking for someone to rest upon and help bring that person into their purpose in life.

The Christian life is not that complicated. It has always been about the partnership between heaven and earth so that the purposes and will of heaven would be displayed and manifested on earth. That is why Jesus asked us to pray and believe it will be answered: *"Your kingdom come, Your will be done on earth as it is in heaven."*

Our primary purpose as a church is always to advance the Kingdom of heaven, by God's grace, for God's glory, through God's Spirit, and that Spirit has been given to every believer, freely and without measure or limitation. Every morning as you rise from your slumber, you have a choice: You can ignore, quench or grieve the Holy Spirit within you, or you can submit to Him, walk in His power and impart Him to those around you throughout that day, wherever you go. It will be that choice, made each and every day by each and every one of us, which will determine if we are being the church that Jesus is building; that church which will finally bring this world to its knees in worship, adoration and submission before the King of Kings and the Lord of Lords.

If you really want to stop 'going to church' and really start 'being the church' then what I have shared with you here is not negotiable. Zechariah said it better than anyone thousands of years ago:

"Not by might nor by power, but by my Spirit," says the Lord Almighty. (Zechariah 4:6)

CHAPTER SIXTEEN
Aligning Ourselves with God

Jesus did not call us to make converts - He called us to make disciples. The word *disciple* means *learner*. You are a disciple of someone and in our context that someone is Jesus. When you stop learning, you stop being a disciple. With discipleship we learn by following. That means we are literally following in the footsteps of another. It's not mimicking or imitating a lifestyle. It's not following a code of ethics. It's actually a relational journey of trust and partnership with another person.

This relational journey of trust is powerfully illustrated in the crucifixion of Jesus. He gave Himself to die. His life wasn't taken from Him, He gave Himself to die. He didn't raise Himself from the dead – God, the Holy Spirit raised Him from the dead. So, just think about this for a moment; when Jesus gave Himself to become sin, He solved the biggest problem in creation.

The devil is a problem for us, but the devil has never been a problem for God. There is not a conflict in the heavens between God and the devil. The devil is a created being, and he can (and will) be destroyed. So, the devil was never the issue - sin was the issue. Sin had only one solution and that was Jesus being born into our world as a human being; living a perfect life without sin; and then becoming the Lamb of God - dying a death we deserved, become an offering for us.

So, picture this if you can: the greatest problem in all of creation is this one little thing called sin and Jesus took that sin upon Himself, so that when the Father poured out His wrath on sin, it actually fell on Jesus. The Bible says, *"The wages of sin is death,"* and that death was embraced for us, by Jesus.

When Jesus offered Himself as an offering for our sin, it was the ultimate expression of trust because when you are dead, you are dead and unless God does something to bring you back to life, you will remain dead. So, Jesus died, trusting that God would raise Him from the dead.

The life of a disciple involves the same trust, and it's a daily decision. The life of a disciple is, *"pick up your cross, and follow me."* It's deciding every day that I'm going to deny what I could do for myself, because I expect at the right time, God will do it. Discipleship is living out the reality of Matthew 6:33, *"... seek first the kingdom of God and His righteousness, and all these things shall be added to you."*

Now throughout history we've done fairly well with one part of the gospel: we know what it is to *"Seek first, the kingdom of God,"* at least in part, and we love to see and hear of people in the body of Christ who have put the King and His kingdom first. So, we know how to seek first the kingdom of God. But we're not always happy with people for whom *"all things are added."* But that's the result of seeking the kingdom first.

We love it when people *"humble themselves under the mighty hand of God."* But we're not always as happy with God when He *"exalts them in due time."* We love hearing stories of people who have given sacrificially in secret. But we're not always as happy with them when they are rewarded in public.

Part of our calling in Christ involves dealing with the issues of jealousy and selfish ambition. Without that death to self, there can be no reward or resurrection. Or to put it another way: my job is to die to self – God's job is the resurrection and reward.

I am not responsible for making sure I get rewarded for all my choices. I am not responsible for God's response, I am only responsible for saying "Yes!" Then I must walk redemptively in relationship, monitoring this part of my life, my inner world, to make sure that jealousy or selfish ambition don't consume my life and destroy my witness.

So, if I see somebody promoted where I thought I should have been promoted, then I have an opportunity for the cross. I learned long ago that I should never turn down an opportunity to die to myself. If we reject an opportunity to die, we reject an opportunity for resurrection and reward. So, discipleship is a relational journey of trust. The one who gives in secret is always rewarded openly in God's time.

Sometimes the people who are criticized most often in the body of Christ because they are outwardly blessed, are actually people who bore a cross in a very difficult situation and the Lord determined to reward them openly. But because we don't always know their back-story, jealousy rises up and masquerades as discernment, giving us information that is illegitimate. Bitterness and jealousy will always provide you with enough information to keep you in deception and it will feel like reason, but it's not. What the cross does in the life of a believer is to go to the root of the issue. So, if you have an ongoing commitment to die to self you will quickly identify jealousy and know it's not discernment. You will see that it's self-promotion and a long way from seeking first the Kingdom.

Matthew 10 is one of the more challenging chapters in the New Testament on the subject of discipleship. The words of Jesus are very confronting, but I love these chapters because I want my wrong thinking to be exposed. Every disciple should read these verses often - otherwise you'll develop a form of Christianity that has nothing to do with the cross. I just want to clarify something here: in actual fact the resurrection is the Christian life, but you can't have a resurrection without a death! Which is why the cross is so central to our faith and our ongoing life as a disciple of Jesus.

> *Anyone who loves their father or mother more than me is not worthy of me; anyone who loves their son or daughter more than me is not worthy of me. Whoever does not take up their cross and follow me is not worthy of me. Whoever finds their life will lose it, and whoever loses their life for my sake will find it.*
> *(Matthew 10:37-39)*

Can you imagine if Jesus were around today, and there was no Bible, and He made a statement like that? Just imagine what social media would do with that! There would be posts all over the internet stating that Jesus wants you to hate your parents and hate your children! I remember hearing a great illustration some time ago about this old man sitting in a rocking chair on his verandah. He is very relaxed, rocking back and forth. On his lap is a very relaxed cat and with each rocking movement the man strokes the cat the wrong way - from the tail towards the head. Somebody sees him doing this one day and says, *"You know you're petting that cat wrong?"* The old man smiles and simply says, *"If he doesn't like it, he can turn around."*

If there are things that Jesus says which you don't like, you'll be the one that has to turn around. You just have to adjust your position until what He says is the obvious expression of a good Father. Until that position is acquired; until you adjust the posture of the heart; a lot of what Jesus says will constantly offend you. He doesn't mind that. What He says will never contradict Scripture - of that we can be confident. But He doesn't mind contradicting our understanding of Scripture. In fact, I think He delights in it.

Jesus also doesn't mind creating conflict within Scripture. In this chapter, He says, *"Don't think I came to bring peace, I came to bring a sword."* But when His birth was announced, the angel said, *"Glory to God in the highest and on earth peace and goodwill towards men."* Both are in fact true. The Bible was written in such a way that it's only understood in the context of a relationship. You can get principles; you can discover a code of ethics for how to live an honest, successful life; you can get that without a relationship. But the full mystery of Scripture is only discerned in the context of a relationship between Jesus and His disciples.

In Proverbs 26:4 it says, *"Do not answer a fool according to his folly, or you yourself will be just like him."* Then the very next verse says, *"Answer a fool according to his folly, or he will be wise in his own eyes."* Which one does He really mean? He doesn't mind creating conflict, because then the only thing we can do is to draw nearer to Him in relationship to find out what He wants in this moment. He creates conflict in thought, as an invitation for us to pursue the One Who holds all mystery. To walk away offended is to miss the point.

When Jesus walked among us as a man, He demonstrated this commitment to a relationship with God. He said He only did what He saw the Father doing and only spoke the words the Father gave Him to speak but how did He know either of those things, as a man? He spent hours in prayer.

Sometimes Jesus withdrew for a whole night to spend time in the presence of the Father. So, when Jesus said, *"If you've seen me, you've seen the Father,"* He was not just stating the objective truth that He was God incarnate. That was certainly true, but as a man, He was saying, *"I have drawn so close to the Father as a human being in relationship with God, that you can see and hear God when you see and hear Me."* This carpenter from Nazareth had drawn near to God and so aligned Himself with God that He could confidently say, *"My heart is God's heart; My dreams are God's dreams; my mission is God's mission; my will is the Father's will."* This was not arrogance, this was simply the fruit of a close, intimate, daily relationship with God.

Therefore, it's one thing for you to say to God, *"I only want what You want – show me Your heart."* That's not a bad prayer to pray at all. But what happens when God answers by saying, *"What do you want?"* That's not something you expected to hear and you are not sure what to say then. *"Me? What do I want? All I want is what You want."* God then replies and says, *"No, that's not the deal. I am trying to shape your heart with My heart and now I want to hear back from you. What's your dream?"* This is hard, so you say it again, *"All I want is just to please you, Lord God - I just want your will."*

Once again, God repeats. *"I no longer call you a servant, I call you a friend and as a friend I want to know what's in your heart?"* But all the time we keep saying, *"Just tell me what to do, Lord. Just give me a list. I'm good at lists – just let me tick off the boxes and please you."* But God is unrelenting here and He says, *"That's what servants do but I have called you My friend. The whole relationship has changed, and I want you to share your heart and dreams and desires with Me as a friend and whatever shaping I do in your life will be done in and through our friendship."*

Whether it's hearing from God, abiding in Christ or aligning ourselves with God in every area of our lives – it all happens in and through our relationship with God, in Christ, by the power of the Spirit. This relational journey of abandonment and trust that is so uncomfortable to many of us is actually the central reality for every genuine disciple. When you are born again into the kingdom of God, He regards you as a son or a daughter and He starts shaping things inside you and before long you will find yourself dreaming of things you never dreamt of before; you find yourself praying about things that never bothered you much before; all of a sudden you start praying certain prayers that you've never prayed in your life, and you don't know where they come from. Well, that is the Lord discipling you. You are praying those prayers and dreaming those dreams because they are in God's heart and as you walk with Him and talk with Him, He reminds you that you are His friend, and He shares His heart with His friends daily until we become the daily expression of His heartbeat. That is what a disciple is.

A disciple embraces the cross - that's our responsibility. The resurrection, the reward, the fruit on the vine is God's job. So, our job is to seek first the Kingdom of God and then God's job is to add all manner of things to us. The challenge of our life is to make sure those things which are added to us do not become our focus – but just a reason to give thanks. The moment we turn our attention away from seeking first the kingdom of God and His righteousness to focus on the rewards of our past choices, it all begins to unravel.

True discipleship is a divine romance; it's a sacred dance; it's a journey of surrender as God takes the lead; it's a daily journey to the cross. It's about embracing the privileged opportunity we have been given which is to die to ourselves and trust God for our resurrection and reward. He says, *"Humble yourself under My mighty hand and I will exalt you in due time."*

I don't ever want to get to a place where the resurrection and reward God gives me turns me away from seeking first the Kingdom to God and His righteousness. In simple terms that means that nothing is held closer to my heart than God Himself. When Jesus said, *"If you love your mum and dad or you love your kids more than you love Me, you're not worthy of Me,"* He wasn't punishing us or encouraging us to be irreverent or inconsiderate or disrespectful toward our family. He was simply saying that, *"If you put Me first in everything, you'll be much more able and empowered to love them as I love them."*

The best thing you could ever do for your family and certainly your children is to put God first. Your love for them will be life-altering if your love for God is the most important thing in your life.

Over my forty plus years in ministry I have probably come across a thousand books, sermons or videos on discipleship. One author or teacher will give us twelve steps to discipleship; another one only has six steps. In fact, there has been so much teaching on discipleship that the whole concept has become overwhelming for many of us in the church. How sad is that? We should not be surprised though.

The enemy of God is always active in the church trying to complicate what is simple. If Satan can turn one task into many and convince us that we are not true disciples until we have ticked all the boxes, then he has won a major victory in his mission to stop us being the church.

When you drill down through all the waffle, all the legalistic rules and requirements and the confusing theological language about discipleship, you find one simple reality: relationship. It's all about our relationship with God. The source of all those wonderful qualities of a good disciple which we are exhorted by well-meaning preachers to achieve through hard work and discipline, is our relationship with God.

We will never align ourselves with God by our hard work, diligence and human effort. We can only align ourselves with God by spending time with Him and getting to know Him as a friend. It's great to worship God as our Creator, Redeemer and deliverer, but His greatest desire and our greatest need is to draw near to Him and enter the 'holy of holies' of His heart – that place where we know we are His friend and even more than that, we are His sons and daughters – He is Abba, Father.

Let me just remind you of three Bible verses which describe this relationship priority better than most verses:

> *"You will seek me and find me when you seek me with all your heart. I will be found by you," declares the Lord ..."*
> *(Jeremiah 29:13-14a)*

I am the vine; you are the branches. If you remain in me and I in you, you will bear much fruit; apart from me you can do nothing. (John 15:5)

"I no longer do I call you servants ... I have called you friends." (John 15:15)

Our greatest need is God Himself. Our greatest desire should be God Himself. Our moment-by-moment responsibility is to die to ourselves and intentionally live for God. We are not called to seek the rewards and blessings of God, we are called to seek God Himself, in His essence. We are not called to produce fruit; we are called to abide in the vine and the fruit will come naturally in the context of relationship.

CHAPTER SEVENTEEN
Embracing our Design

There are a lot of people who have this notion that Jesus came to earth to plead on our behalf, to calm down an angry Father that was looking for somebody to punish - but Jesus actually came to do the opposite. He came to reveal a Father Who was passionate for His people. Now in the context in which we live today, there's a secularization of our culture happening which is working very hard to remove the concept of a creator completely. When you get rid of a creator, you get rid of the designer. With no designer, you get rid of design, because you can't have design without a designer. When you don't have design then you're free to do whatever you want and that's where Satan wants us to be.

From that first encounter with the human race in the Garden of Eden, Satan has consistently been telling us we are free to do whatever we want, without consequence. Design implies that when God created us with design, He created us with purpose. Purpose carries with it, the implication of destiny, and destiny carries with it responsibility and accountability. So, the bottom line is this: the epic effort to destroy the concept of a creator, a designer, is meant to erase that which we were born with, that conviction that I must give an account of my life.

When God created the world, He filled it with all kinds of animals to reproduce after their kind. There are two laws in creation that actually reveal part of why Jesus needed to come. Number one, we reproduce after our kind: if you plant a flower seed, you don't grow a horse, it reproduces after its kind. Within each species, there's latitude, but there's no crossing over without consequence. If you mate a male donkey with a female horse, you get a mule. But that mule cannot reproduce because it is outside God's design. Scientists have actually discovered a vital chromosome which is missing in mules. It is in God's design that we reproduce, that we are fruitful - not just in producing other humans but in becoming productive contributors to society.

That's who we are. In one of Jesus' parables, He talks about ten servants who were given a sum of money, they in turn reinvested it, and the master came back to collect the profits. To the one who increased his one talent to ten, the Master said, *"Now be in charge of ten cities, enter into the joy of your master."* The main point of that parable is that responsibility is our access to greater joy, greater responsibility. Joy is not something you get by doing nothing. It's something you get by functioning according to your design. Design is what connects us to purpose and to truly be the Church we must learn to embrace our unique design.

Each and every one of us has something to contribute to the overall story of mankind that no one else can contribute. There's a uniqueness in every person. We were all made in the image of God and when you destroy the concept of design and purpose, you erase the sense of accountability for illustrating who God is. Sin, therefore, is when we operate outside of our design. We are designed by God and in God's image - anything outside of the nature and character of God is sin.

Another part of God's creation is what the book of Genesis calls *'seed time and harvest.'* In other words, *'you reap what you sow.'* You plant a seed and it will bring forth fruit. If I sow a thousand acres of corn, I'm going to have a harvest of corn. If I sow mercy, I will reap mercy. The law of *'seed time and harvest'* is written into the DNA of all creation. What you plant you will harvest; what you sow you will reap. Sadly, this also applies to sin. If you sow hatred, bitterness, dishonesty, violence, deception or selfishness, you will reap all the bad fruit and consequences of that seed at harvest time. Now that was the reality into which God came to earth and took upon human flesh in Jesus.

Jesus stepped into this broken world to stop the flow of sowing and reaping which came from our sin. He actually took upon Himself all the bad fruit from our wrongdoing. He took upon Himself what we deserved so that we could receive what He deserved. That's what salvation is. It's not just a temporary postponement of sin and judgement. Jesus actually took upon Himself the punishment we deserved for all sin, past, present and future. He did that so we can receive the life He deserved.

That's the wonder of the incarnation. The most confronting reality is that this 'master reset' in us could only be achieved through the death of Jesus. He came to do many things, but ultimately, He came to die.

> *And he died for all, that those who live should no longer live for themselves but for him who died for them and was raised again. So, from now on we regard no one from a worldly point of view. Though we once regarded Christ in this way, we do so no longer. Therefore, if anyone is in Christ, the new creation has come. The old has gone, the new is here!*
> *(2 Corinthians 5:15-17)*

The last thing we needed was some kind of soothing ointment over the open wound of sin. We didn't need a spiritual band-aid placed over a problem. Sin permeated everything and impacted everyone and it caused us all to walk away from our design, our destiny, our purpose. But worse than all that, sin caused us to walk away from the Designer, our Creator, our loving heavenly Father. Therefore, everything needed to change. We needed a new start, a whole new beginning. In Genesis 1 we read about the creation of all things and how on the seventh day God rested. Since that time, there has never been anything new created until Jesus died and was raised from the dead. Then everyone who puts their faith in Him, the Bible says, is born again. In that born again experience, they become something that has never existed before - a new creation.

When we are born again into Christ, we are given the ability once more to grow into the fullness of what God designed us to be. In that context, we bring a fruitfulness to the planet through our life. All of that is impossible without the grace of God. It's impossible without a miracle of God unfolding in our lives.

> *All this is from God, who reconciled us to himself through Christ and gave us the ministry of reconciliation: that God was reconciling the world to himself in Christ, not counting people's sins against them. And he has committed to us the message of reconciliation. (2 Corinthians 5:18-19)*

I want you to say these words out loud: *God has given me the ministry of reconciliation.* That is actually true for every disciple of Jesus Christ, no matter how old or young. It's a mandate. Once you have been reconciled to God, it's in your new nature is to be a reconciler. You are to produce after your own kind. You are to bear fruit from the tree into which you have been grafted.

> *We are therefore Christ's ambassadors, as though God were making his appeal through us. We implore you on Christ's behalf: Be reconciled to God. God made him who had no sin to be sin for us, so that in him we might become the righteousness of God.*
> *(2 Corinthians 5:20-21)*

Jesus came; lived a perfect life as a human; faced every kind of temptation a human can face, yet He did not yield to any of them in the slightest measure. He became a Lamb that had no blemish and was not defiled. There was absolutely nothing wrong with this Lamb, so He became the perfect offering. Why? Because this cycle of sowing and reaping would go on destroying people for eternity unless someone stopped it. We were powerless to stop it - all of humanity was caught up in the vicious 'sow and reap' reality. So, Jesus stepped into the middle of that mess and basically said, *"Let the harvest they all deserve – now come to me."*

> *MERCY is when I don't get what I deserve.*
>
> *GRACE is when I get what I don't deserve.*

So can you see, this is not an angry father looking to destroy His people. This is a loving Father who was willing to sacrifice His only Son, Who stepped into this 'cause and effect' creation and willingly bore the fruit, reaped the harvest from the sin which had consumed us all.

God's design for His whole creation, requires productivity, increase, reproducing after its kind, sowing and reaping; it's the way you and I come into life. If He changes those basic laws of creation, He changes the way we will also find breakthrough, maturity, progress. Jesus therefore embraced the punishment, the consequences for all that was wrong with us.

Then Jesus turns to us and says, *"You are now reconciled to God and I have given you the ministry of reconciliation. Go and tell others the truth so I might reconcile them to the Father also."* What is that truth? It's right here in one of the most confronting, powerful, amazing verses in the whole Bible – a verse which contains the very essence of the gospel. *"For He (the Father) made Him (the Son) who knew no sin, to be sin for us, that we might become the righteousness of God in Him." (v.21)*

What a truly amazing statement: *"That we might become the righteousness of God in Him."* What an incredible reality. This is the gospel: God made Jesus, Who knew no sin personally, to become sin so that the real sinners, the ones who rebelled against God and did whatever they pleased, would be restored to our proper condition, our original design, our Creator's image, and therefore become the righteousness of God.

Only then can we become equipped disciples who embrace the mission of Christ, the ministry of reconciliation. Only then are we able live as our Creator and Designer intended. Only then is the church Jesus promised to build, equipped and ready to complete His mission on earth. Only then are we truly 'being the church.' God's design for us is that we live in perfect harmony with Him and that we live and move and have our very being in Christ, through Christ and for Christ.

All that comes as a free gift. That free gift comes to us in love, with no strings attached, no requirements, no religious hoops we have to jump through. It's a mysterious, wonderful, outrageous and dangerously free gift. Your favour before God and your right standing with God is not in any way determined by your personal performance – and just as well – because if it was, then your performance would have to be absolute 100% perfection, because even the tiniest sin would destroy you in the presence of a pure, holy God. Your eternal relationship with God has been secured by God Himself. He wouldn't trust you with something so important to Him.

On our smart phones and computers today, we have an option to reset the device and 'restore factory settings.' Well, that is exactly what God did for us and only God could do it. He restored our default settings; our original design; our intended purpose - and He did it all in and through the birth, life, death and resurrection of Jesus Christ.

This is the gospel! This is the Truth! Believe it, receive it and watch it transform your life. This is why every man, woman and young person on this planet pays homage to this Christ every time they write the date. This is why our hospitals, our schools, our judicial system, our governments all have their roots in the community of faith which this Man birthed when He allowed Himself to be nailed to a tree. This is why all the armies that have ever marched; all the navies that have ever sailed; all the parliaments that have ever sat; all the kings that ever reigned put together, have not affected mankind on earth as powerfully as this one solitary life.

When sin entered our perfect world, everything broke and all of creation has been groaning ever since to be put right - to be reset, rebooted, restored to its original purpose. Only the One Who made us and designed us could press that reset button and He did that through the most outrageous act of love and grace.

God made him who had no sin to be sin[a] for us, so that in him we might become the righteousness of God. (2 Corinthians 5:21)

You and I have been reborn, reset, renewed, restored and reconciled to our Creator, our Designer our heavenly Father. That is our design and the degree to which we embrace our design will impact our ability to truly be the Church Jesus birthed and promised to build.

CHAPTER EIGHTEEN
Loving God

We love because he first loved us. (1 John 4:19)

With just those seven words, John encapsulates one of the most important and foundational truths in the Christian faith and if we are serious about being fully equipped as Jesus' disciples; if truly want to be the church, then this truth must dominate our thinking, our worldview, our understanding of the gospel and our purpose in life. *We love because He first loved us.* That means that I can only love God in the measure I receive love from God. Receiving the love of God gives me a capacity for love I did not have before. I was designed to be a lover of God. I was designed to love God with everything that I am - every part of my being. The Bible says I'm to love God with all my heart, all my soul, all my mind and all my strength. Everything about my spirit man is geared up and ready to love God completely.

Perhaps you've heard someone being described as being, *'so heavenly minded, they're of no earthly use.'* Maybe you have said that of someone. Well, I have to say that's a really stupid thing to say. It's also a contradiction because the only way you can be of any earthly use is to be heavenly minded. If I am not heavenly minded, I am missing the whole point of life. I am to love God with all my heart, soul, mind and strength. There's an emotional capacity to love that must find expression in my relationship with God and that is a life-long journey. I never stop to grade myself - I just keep going forward. I'm just loving with all my heart and soul – but also my mind. The intellect is actually at its finest when it considers God. *'The fool says in his heart, there is no God.'* (Psalm 14:1)

We are designed for love and first and foremost that is love for God. We were hard-wired to love God – that's our design - but the culture around us is trying really hard to erase the whole concept of design. It's not just sexual orientation or gender that's under fire - it's life itself that's being re-defined by our culture.

I was born to be loved by God and to love God in return. Now part of that expression of my love for God needs to be seen and measured in my love for others. If I say I love God but don't demonstrate love towards others, you have every reason to question my love for God because there's no evidence. In other words, spiritual realities have to be measurable in the natural. Spiritual realities have to manifest or bear fruit in our day-to-day life on earth.

Let me stress this again, there has been a war raging now for over a hundred years to remove the concept of a creator. If there's no creator, then there's no design - because you can't have design without a designer. You can't say the beaver has teeth that were designed in such a way so it could chew through trees. You cannot use the word design if there's no designer. There's no such thing as random design.

Design has to be intentional – it has to have a designer. So, if I remove the key concept of a creator, a designer; if there is no design, then there is no purpose; if there is no purpose, there is no destiny; if there is no destiny, there is no accountability. Welcome to our world!

This war in our culture is trying to undermine the absolute necessity of wisdom because giving an account of my life is at the very heart of true biblical wisdom. I will stand before God one day and give an account. So once that truth is erased from the consciousness of humanity then things become frightening. Everything becomes random and is driven by self-absorption, self-protection and self-promotion.

The truth is, I have been created and designed to love God with all my heart, soul and mind. But I am also designed to love God with all my strength. This is not talking about our physical strength. I doubt it means you sing worship songs while you lift weights. This is talking about loving God with our whole body.

> *How lovely is your dwelling place, Lord Almighty! My soul yearns, even faints, for the courts of the Lord; my heart and my flesh cry out for the living God. (Psalm 84:1-2)*

My heart and my flesh, that is my whole body cries out for God. We know what physical appetites are. We know what it is to be thirsty. We know what it is to hunger for food. Well, it's actually possible to spend time in the glorious presence of God where your body becomes recalibrated to hunger for what it was born for: God Himself. Every human being was designed by God - for God. That means every part of us - our mind; our emotions; our will; our physical body; our gifts and talents – it was all designed by God, for God.

In our encounter of loving God and receiving love from God, the perfection of our design is revealed. When every part of me burns for God – then I am at my very best. This is what the Apostle Paul was trying to explain in Ephesians 3:19 when he exhorted us, "*... to know this love that surpasses knowledge.*" We are to know by experience what is beyond our comprehension.

It's tragic but true that our modern culture and lifestyle makes it impossible for us to fully embrace the love of God. We are just too busy, and busyness is artificial significance. Busyness insulates us from being still enough to be loved. I don't mean God doesn't love you when you're busy - God's love is constant and immeasurable. But when your life is so full, you are not able to discover, experience or embrace the full dimension of God's love. If ever there was a verse for our generation it has to be Psalm 46:10, "*Be still and know that I am God.*" Stillness is something our whole culture seems to despise.

I'm not saying you can't learn in the midst of hectic activity; we all do. But there's something about being still in the presence of God that takes us to a very different place. This is when people receive some of their best insights, inspiration and 'moments' in God.

For example, when you're sleeping, or just waking up – your defenses are down, anxiety hasn't kicked in, your agenda hasn't come to mind - in that place of stillness, you can often see and hear and embrace God in a way you never can in the hustle and bustle of the rest of the day. Setting aside time to be still in the presence of God is so important. What is even more tragic is when our busyness actually is for God.

This is so evident in the modern church in the western world. Our very full agenda for God will often insulate us from God. We consume so much but we fail to grow.

> ". . though by this time you ought to be teachers, you need someone to teach you the elementary truths of God's word all over again. You need milk, not solid food! Anyone who lives on milk, being still an infant, is not acquainted with the teaching about righteousness. But solid food is for the mature, who by constant use have trained themselves to distinguish good from evil."
> (Hebrews 5:12-14)

God's Word is divided in two categories in this passage, milk and meat. Milk comforts and soothes, and it is meant for babies. Meat is the word of righteousness, that which provokes change, and it is for maturing adults. If I only search the Scriptures to find milk, then I will live in comfort, I will live in perpetual immaturity, because it's the word of righteousness that provokes me and brings me into change and growth into maturity. Those who partake of this solid food have their senses exercised or trained to discern good and evil. All our physical senses: smell, sight, hearing, touch and taste, were designed in us to recognize God. I know it sounds mystical, but the writer of Hebrews is basically saying, having your senses trained to discern good and evil is a requirement of a teacher. For though you ought to have been teachers by now, you don't yet have your senses trained in the kingdom of God. Listening is the key in God's kingdom.

I believe there's this intensely glorious harmony and melody woven into everything that exists in the kingdom of God. There's colour, there's beauty, there's sound, there's light and everything has a divine purpose. There are colours that have never even been thought of by us. There are sounds there which have never been heard by a human ear. I think worship leaders, musicians, and song writers more and more are going to be hearing sounds and melodies God has kept hidden. Sounds which only exist in God's world but are occasionally heard by people. I personally think Handel's Messiah is one of those pieces. This man was very obnoxious, angry and impatient - not a godly man at all. But one day Handel was given a poem written by a young poet. The one place this angry, unpleasant man had a soft spot in his heart was for young poets. So, Handel took this poem, and he began to read over it. As he did, he began to hear sounds he had never heard before. So, he began to write. He would write nonstop for hours and hours. He seemed to be obsessed with completing this project. The woman who cooked meals for him would come in to feed him and he'd turn her away lest he lost his connection to these sounds he had never heard before.

He wrote and wrote and wrote and the result was *Handel's Messiah* - an incredible piece of music - lyrics by a young unknown poet; music from a master who tapped into heavenly sounds. He penned something that is sung by millions of people around the world still today – many of them are unbelievers! I think only God can pull that off. But that's not the end of this story. When Handel was done, he was not the same man. He became the most godly, gentle, gracious, kind man you could ever imagine meeting because he had heard the sounds of heaven and captured them for all to hear, until the end of time.

Therefore, there are things being spoken in the heavenly realm we don't usually hear – especially when we are so busy, and our lives are so full of activities and tasks. Jesus heard those things, and He spoke them into our world and many people were stunned. They said, *"We've never heard teaching like this before."* That's because they were hearing a heavenly sound. When Jesus spoke, it recalibrated the hearts of people. Suddenly, people began to adjust their thoughts and lives to make sure they were in line with what God was saying.

'My heart and my flesh cry out for the living God.' I am to love God with all my heart, my soul, my mind, and my strength. The person who has no control over their thoughts, has little ability to love God with their mind. Our mind needs to be clear enough to love God with our intellect.

If you set your mind on heavenly things, not earthly things, then you can capture God's heartbeat, you can behold the wonder of His excellence, His majesty and His amazing grace.

The more I can embrace that reality, the more it becomes part of my expression of love. But if I get filled with fear, worry, and anxiety, then I will become disengaged from my capacity for love. Sometimes, I will sit in my office and take a moment to put every concern, every responsibility, every worry about anything aside, and just sit there and just say, *"Father, I'm here to be loved by you."* I don't become anxious over what I might be seeing or discerning or feeling. I am not here to make anything happen – just to receive. God doesn't need my cooperation at this point - just my silence. So, I sit there with nothing to do, nothing to say except, *"God. I know you love me. So, I'm going to sit here and just receive your love."* In five minutes, I get up and I know something is happening in my heart. I know I am engaging with God at a level of intimacy I could never have created myself.

I believe the Lord is wanting to teach us how to be free in our affection for Him. This is what being still and knowing He is God looks like. It's an intentional focus on our part and the more we do this, the more we learn. We will thinking will be better and clearer. Our courage will be greater. Our faith will be stronger. Our affection for Him will rise more each day. The Scriptures come alive as we embrace the truth of God's Word. Here is another one for your fridge door: *It's not true because it's in the Bible. It's in the Bible, because it's true.*

> *Hear, O Israel: The Lord our God, the Lord is one. Love the Lord your God with all your heart and with all your soul and with all your strength. These commandments that I give you today are to be on your hearts. Impress them on your children. Talk about them when you sit at home and when you walk along the road, when you lie down and when you get up. Tie them as symbols on your hands and bind them on your foreheads. Write them on the doorframes of your houses and on your gates. (Deut. 6:4-9)*

This word of God is not given to us as mere commandments. We are privileged to have the whole revelation of God. We have the New Testament. We live this side of the cross of Christ. So, the main difference between the Old and New Testament as I see it is simply this: in the Old Testament we are commanded to do things; in the New Testament we are empowered to do what we've been commanded to do. Law requires - grace enables. The law is holy, but the law can never make you holy. Only God can do that, in and through the life, death and resurrection of Jesus Christ.

In the Old Testament we are all commanded to love God with our whole being. That could never happen until one man, Jesus Christ, fulfilled that command perfectly, as a man, and then gifted us that perfect performance by His grace. Jesus scored 100% in all areas of His life as a human being and then He wrote our name on His report card and handed it to the Father and said, *"It is finished."* So now, because of His great love, which is poured out upon us, we too can love Him. Now we end where we began with John's foundational truth, *"We love because he first loved us."* (1 John 4:19).

You can only love God in the measure you receive love from God. Receiving the love of God gives you a capacity for love you did not have before. When God delivered you from the kingdom of darkness and brought you into the kingdom of his Son, Jesus Christ, you were born again, your spirit was regenerated by the Holy Spirit, so that now, everything about you from God's perspective is already geared up to love God completely. Only as we touch heaven, can we change the earth.

I am sure you will agree that our earthly world is in serious need of change. Our cities, our nation and the whole world is crying out for healing, for restoration, for reconciliation, for harmony, for peace, for faith, hope and love. All of that and more is possible when the people of God get serious about touching heaven, changing earth, in Christ, through Christ, for Christ. That all begins as we open up to the love of God and allow Him to transform us into the image of His Son, our Saviour, the Lord Jesus Christ. All of heaven is waiting for you and me to make that choice each moment of each day. When that happens, we will finally know what it is to be the church – and all heaven will break lose as we are equipped to fulfill the mission of Christ, by His grace and for His glory.

CHAPTER NINETEEN
Christ in our Midst

I think most of us have grown up knowing that the church is not a building. From the day the church was born and for the next couple of centuries, there were no buildings and no thought of having any. Many believe that was the best time in the church's history. We know that the church is actually the people of God wherever they are, whatever label they carry; they are the disciples of Christ across the nation and around the world. The church spans all nationalities, all ethnic groupings and all geographical locations. Then there is the local expression of the church – individual congregations and even small groups of believers - we are the church Jesus promised to build.

Getting our thinking right about the nature of the church and some key concepts in the kingdom of God is very important. It's just as important we get it right when we think about the purpose of the church. Now we have all heard and read what we call *the Great Commission*. That's when Jesus told us to go and make disciples of all nations. But what many of us don't know is that in the Greek, the active verb in that verse is not *go* - it's actually the word for *make disciples*. So, the verse actually means, *"as you go (or in your going) make disciples ..."* In other words, this commission is really, *"In your normal coming and going throughout your whole life, make disciples!"*

I believe our Lord is always wanting to equip the church to fulfill that commission and show us all where the true strength of the church lies. Now I love large gatherings of God's people. The largest one I have been part of was many years ago in the Brisbane Entertainment Centre and I will never forget how good it was to worship with over 13,000 brothers and sisters all in the one place. At a local church level, I have pastored congregations from 5 to 500 and everything in between and they have all been special experiences. In this current season, I believe the Lord is wanting us to re-discover what the early church knew from the beginning and that is the true strength of the church lies in the two or three committed disciples gathering in His name. Large gatherings are great – it's good to know we belong to something bigger and more significant than our little world of influence. That's important.

But authentic discipleship always begins in our own heart as individuals and manifests in the intimacy of 2-3 people gathered in Jesus' name, worshipping, learning, praying, and growing in grace. We wrongly think that power comes in numbers. Power always comes from Jesus, transforming hearts one by one.

> *When Jesus came to the region of Caesarea Philippi, he asked his disciples, "Who do people say the Son of Man is?" They replied, "Some say John the Baptist; others say Elijah; and still others, Jeremiah or one of the prophets." "But what about you?" he asked. "Who do you say I am?" Simon Peter answered, "You are the Messiah, the Son of the living God.*
>
> *Jesus replied, "Blessed are you, Simon son of Jonah, for this was not revealed to you by flesh and blood, but by my Father in heaven. And I tell you that you are Peter, and on this rock, I will build my church, and the gates of Hades will not overcome it. I will give you the keys of the kingdom of heaven; whatever you bind on earth will be bound in heaven, and whatever you loose on earth will be loosed in heaven." (Matthew 16:13-19)*

In the NASB translation, verse 19 reads, *"Whatever you bind on earth shall have been bound in heaven."* In the NIV and many other translations, that it just a footnote to read if you can be bothered. But it's actually a more accurate translation and it's more correct theologically.

Jesus taught that we are to manifest the reality of heaven on earth – to mirror that reality here and that is the overall theme in all of Jesus' teaching. You can't change reality in the eternal kingdom of heaven by your actions in this earthly kingdom – but you can reflect what happens in heaven and change the world around you. That's exactly what Jesus meant when He told us to pray, *"Your kingdom come, your will be done on earth as it is in heaven."*

So, the backbone of the Great Commission for every believer is learning how to partner with God to bring the reality of His reign, His dominion and His kingdom into the specific areas of our human experience in the kingdom of this world. Touching heaven, changing earth – in Christ, through Christ, for Christ.

Jesus then turns to His disciples and says, *"Who do you say that I am?"* Peter answered and said, *"You are the Christ, the Son of the living God."* Jesus responded, *"Blessed are you Simon Barjona, because flesh and blood did not reveal this to you, but My Father who is in heaven."* Jesus was pointing out that something significant just happened. Heaven invaded earth and it happened through one person speaking God's truth. Truth from the kingdom of God was just spoken in our kingdom by one human being.

Jesus then said that it's upon that rock – Peter's confession that Jesus is the Christ, the Son of the living God – upon that rock, Jesus is going to build His church. It is the personal revelation of Jesus as the Messiah, the truth that He is the Son of the living God - that is what the church is built upon and that revelation comes to individuals one by one.

Think about this. The church is built upon revelation. The essence of your faith is that God revealed something to you, and you responded. There is no salvation apart from the revelation of God. *"Man does not live by bread alone, but by every word that proceeds from the mouth of God."* (Matthew 4:4) There is this life continuously flowing in us and through us because of God's revelation – because we hear from God. Now it's important to be truthful and humble here and admit that we don't always hear from God clearly. Our own thoughts and desires and wonky ideas can often get in the way. But we are on a journey to increase our capacity, our ability to perceive what God is saying and doing in and around us.

Part of the problem we have is that God's first language is not English, or Spanish, or whatever other languages humans speak. God reveals Himself and His Word in a myriad of ways and He gives us the discernment to perceive, to comprehend and to apprehend and embrace His word. So here, God gives Peter the discernment to know that Jesus is the Christ, the Son of the living God and then Jesus immediately says, *"You just heard from the Father and the truth you just spoke will be the foundation of the church I am going to build."*

Then Jesus really blows the minds of the disciples in verse 19 when He says, *"I will give you the keys of the kingdom of heaven; and whatever you bind on earth shall have been bound in heaven, and whatever you loose on earth shall have been loosed in heaven."*

This is a very significant assignment that Jesus gives to every one of us as individuals. Now if we skip forward to Matthew chapter 18, we see the same statement from Jesus but He goes on to say more: says, but then He goes on and says this,

> *Truly I tell you, whatever you bind on earth will be bound in heaven, and whatever you loose on earth will be loosed in heaven. Again, truly I tell you that if two of you on earth agree about anything they ask for, it will be done for them by my Father in heaven. For where two or three gather in my name, there am I with them."* (Matthew 18:19-20)

Now when the Lord said, *"I will build my church ..."* He did not use a term that would have been very commonplace in Jewish culture at that time. He did not say *synagogue* or *temple*. The word used here is *ecclesia* and it's an important word to understand.

Ecclesia referred to a group of two or three people who are citizens of a particular country, or government. Whenever they gathered together, they actually represented the government of the country they were from. So, if you had Roman citizens that were in Greece and they worked together, say at a bakery, and they got together at lunchtime and talked together, they were actually representing the government of Rome. That's the term that is used here.

Jesus used a secular term, but I don't really think He was borrowing from the secular world, I think He was taking back what He inspired them to think and to do in the first place. He did this also by using the term Apostle, which was a Greek and eventually a Roman term. That's what He did here with the word *ecclesia*.

Jesus says that when two or three of us gather in His name, He is there in our midst. The presence of God is the mark of divine authority, and this is the backbone of our assignment to disciple the nations. This is not an optional extra. This is the heart and soul of how you and I were designed. We were designed and then assigned by God to be on this great planet as citizens of another world. As a citizen of that world, I am to look for the one or two others with whom I can meet and come into a place of agreement, so that the manifest presence of God will settle upon our gathering together. Then in that position, we touch heaven and change earth; we take what is real in God's kingdom and make it real in this kingdom; we make decisions that actually shape the course of human history. That's why Jesus could say what He did in John 15:7, *"If you remain in me and my words remain in you, ask whatever you wish, and it will be done for you."*

So, you see that any lack of answers to prayer is not ever a problem on God's part. The lack of answers is a problem on our end, and it's related to our ability or willingness to truly abide in Christ. The felt presence of God is the absolute key to continuous answers to prayer and living apart from that; doing our best to mimic God's will; doing our best to pray for things that we think ought to happen - just won't work. It's not that our prayers are wrong necessarily, it's not that what we've requested is against God's will, we are just missing the strength of abiding in Christ.

When we have the manifest presence of God upon us and we come before the Father with a request, there is a spiritual reality into which we have been invited - *"Abide in me, let my words abide in you."* It's the acknowledged, felt presence of God. It's not just a recognition of the Almighty God being here, it is our actual engagement with Him.

Abiding is an engaged participation with a person, where there is an encounter; there is an exchange; there is a fellowship; there is an intimacy; there is a connection that is otherworldly. In that connection, we are positioned to think differently, to feel differently, to see differently and if we are sitting with another brother or sister, family member or whoever, then Jesus says in that context the weight of the government of His world is upon our shoulders. That is the reason we can bind anything here that is already bound there. In that position, we are much more prone to see and discern the reality of God's world.

King David made an interesting statement in Psalm 16:8 when he said, *"I have set the Lord always before me: because he is at my right hand, I shall not be moved."* What did he mean here? Well, he doesn't mean we can grab hold of God and put Him where we want. He wasn't saying that. I believe what he was saying is this: since you can't imagine a place where God isn't, you might as well believe He is with you. If we believe God is everywhere, that must include here, right now, with me.

What is abiding in Christ? It is acknowledging the presence of God who is with you to a point of engagement, relationship, awareness. Something happens in that heartfelt connection with the presence of God, the Spirit of God, Who is with me and will never leave me, so that I live more aware of what He wants; I live more conscious of His will; I live more aware of His heart and, little by little, my heart is re-programmed, my mind is renewed, my spirit is aligned with His Spirit. That is abiding in Christ.

So, I have a dream and it is as bold as Martin Luther King's dream in 1964; I have a dream that very soon the people of God across our nation will finally get to the point where we are sick and tired of letting the enemy have his way. I dream that we will all see the truth together and affirm that we are here representing another world, in fact we are representing God Himself, and the Governor of that world is here, present with us.

In this dream, God's people decide to finally connect their heart to His; they decide to live aware of Him and all that He is; the words that He breathes; until we finally think what He thinks, want what He wants, and dream what He dreams. Then finally that abiding presence becomes the primary influence in our conscious and unconscious mind. In my dream I see two or three people in prayer here and another two or three over there and still more in the workplace, in hospitals, in every corner or our communities – hundreds and thousands of people manifesting the simplicity and the power of *ecclesia* – God, in the midst of His people.

Off the west coast of Scotland is a small group of islands called the Hebrides. Between 1949 and 1952 a widespread revival swept through these islands in answer to the prayers of God's people. Instrumental in this revival was the evangelist, Duncan Campbell. He came to the Isle of Lewis to conduct a two-week evangelistic campaign and ended up staying two years!

It was a massive revival which touched tens of thousands of people and impacted a whole generation for years to come. But like many outpourings of God, this all began when two or three gathered.

In a small cottage by the roadside in the village of Barvas lived two elderly sisters, Peggy and Christine Smith. They were eighty-four and eighty-two years old. Peggy was blind and her sister was doubled over with arthritis. Unable to attend public worship any longer, their humble cottage became a sanctuary where they met with God. To them came the promise: "*I will pour water upon him that is thirsty and floods upon the dry ground,*" and they pleaded this day and night in prayer.

One night Peggy had a revelation: revival was coming, and the church of her fathers would be crowded again with young people! She sent for the Minister at that time, the Rev. James Murray MacKay, and told him what God had shown her, asking him to call his elders and deacons together for special times of waiting upon God.

In the same district a group of men praying in a barn also experienced a foretaste of coming blessing. One night as they waited upon God, a young deacon rose and read part of the twenty-fourth Psalm:

> *Who may ascend the mountain of the Lord? Who may stand in his holy place? The one who has clean hands and a pure heart, who does not trust in an idol or swear by a false god. They will receive blessing from the Lord. (Psalm 24:3-5a)*

Turning to the others he said: "*Brethren, it seems to me just so much humbug to be waiting and praying as we are, if we ourselves are not rightly related to God.*" Then lifting his hands toward heaven, he cried: "*Oh God, are my hands clean? Is my heart pure?*" He got no further but fell prostrate to the floor. An awareness of God filled the barn, and a stream of supernatural power was let lose in their lives. They had moved into a new sphere of God awareness, believing implicitly in the promise of revival.

Before we leave Peggy and her sister, another story must be told which further illustrates the holy intimacy the Lord desires to have with us. When the movement was at its height, Peggy sent for Duncan Campbell, asking him to go to a small, isolated village to hold a meeting. The people of this village did not favour the revival and had already made clear their policy of non-involvement. Duncan explained the situation to Peggy and told her that he questioned the wisdom of her request. "*Besides,*" he added, "*I have no leadings to go to that place.*" She turned in the direction of his voice, her sightless eyes seemed to penetrate his soul. "*Mr. Campbell, if you were living as near to God as you ought to be, He would reveal His secrets to you also.*"

Duncan felt like a subordinate being reprimanded for defying his general. He humbly accepted the rebuke as from the Lord and asked if he and Mr. MacKay could spend the morning in prayer with them. She agreed, and later as they knelt together in the cottage, Peggy prayed: "*Lord, You remember what You told me this morning, that in this village You are going to save seven men who will become pillars in the church of my fathers. Lord, I have given Your message to Mr. Campbell and it seems he is not prepared to receive it. Oh Lord, give him wisdom, because he badly needs it!*"

"*All right, Peggy, I'll go to the village,*" said Duncan when they had finished praying. She replied, "*You'd better! And God will give you a congregation.*" Arriving in the village at seven o'clock they found a large bungalow crowded to capacity with many people assembled outside waiting for God to move. When Duncan had finished preaching, a minister beckoned him to the end of the house to speak again to a number of people who were mourning over their sins. Duncan entered the room and was not surprised at all to find seven men (Peggy's seven men!) each of whom embraced the gospel and accepted the Lord that night. When two or three gather ... mighty things can happen.

One more story: It was always evident how much Billy Graham loved and respected his father, Frank. He was a dairy farmer in Charlotte, North Carolina, who almost lost everything in the Great Depression but managed to slowly recover and leave a legacy of faith, hard work and determination. In May 1934, Billy Graham was just a lanky, mischievous teenager when his father and a group of local men gathered under a grove of shade trees at the edge of a pasture on the Grahams' dairy farm. They had met several times before - always outdoors - at different locations around Charlotte to pray for God to send revival to their city, their state and beyond.

Billy Graham was fifteen years old and doing his afternoon chores in the barn when his father and a small group of local businessmen prayed for God to raise up someone who would take the Gospel to the ends of the earth. But this particular May prayer gathering is still being talked about almost 90 years later. That's because at this meeting, as Frank Graham recalled later, a paper salesman named Vernon Patterson suggested a bold new prayer: that God would raise up someone from Charlotte, North Carolina, who would take the Gospel to the ends of the earth.

The day his father joined the others in their bold new prayer, the Gospel was likely the farthest thing from young Billy's mind. That changed just six months later when a traveling evangelist, Dr. Mordecai Ham, caught the attention of this gangly, blue-eyed teenager. It wasn't easy to get young Billy Graham to set foot inside the tent where Dr. Ham was preaching night after night, but he eventually decided to see what all the fuss was about. It was at that tent meeting on November 1st, 1934 - just six days before Billy Graham's 16th birthday - that the future 'Evangelist to the World' and 'Pastor to Presidents' embraced Jesus Christ as his Saviour and Lord and the rest is history!

Both Billy Graham and his father gave all the glory to God, Who answered a sincere prayer from a group of men on a dairy farm in 1934. When two or three gather ... with God in their midst ... things happen!

CHAPTER TWENTY
The Dwelling Place of God

What is the church? How can believers 'be' the church instead of just 'go' to church? Such are the questions we've been wrestling with throughout this book. They are simple questions, but the answers are not always simple and there is no single answer. There are many things we should do (and stop doing), believe (and stop believing) in order to truly be the church Jesus birthed and promised to build.

The problem with many Christians is that they have a low 'ecclesiology,' that is a low understanding of what the church is and their role within it. For many of us, being the church simply means that we call ourselves Christians and attend various church activities on a regular or semi-regular basis. But outside of that we may have no real commitment to or investment in the church of Jesus Christ. If we don't fully understand the purpose of something then it is destined for misuse or neglect. I believe that is exactly what has been happening in the modern church. This is not new - there was something of this happening in the early church and Paul addresses it in his letter to the Ephesians.

> *Consequently, you are no longer foreigners and aliens, but fellow citizens with God's people and members of God's household, built on the foundation of the apostles and prophets, with Christ Jesus himself as the chief cornerstone. In him the whole building is joined together and rises to become a holy temple in the Lord. And in him you too are being built together to become a dwelling in which God lives by his Spirit. (Ephesians 2:19-22)*

In the preceding verses (11-18), Paul calls for the Gentiles to remember their past when they were hated by the Jews, called *'the uncircumcision'* and without citizenship in Israel; without covenants; without hope; without Christ and without God. The Jews were called to be a holy nation that drew the other nations towards God. However, they became prideful in their position as God's people and instead of ministering to the Gentiles - they despised them. There was tremendous animosity between the two groups. But through His life, death and resurrection, Jesus Christ brought these two hostile groups together before God. He made them one people - one body. He made them His church.

It seems that Paul addressed this because there was still division in the early church. Though they were saved and part of Christ's body, they weren't really being the church. In Romans chapter 14, Paul writes about divisions over eating meat offered to idols, practicing the Sabbath day and other things that divided Jew and Gentile Christians. Even the apostle Peter would not eat with Gentiles when certain Jews were around (Galatians 2). They started to form separate Jewish and Gentile congregations. Many in the early church did not fully understand what Christ had done for them and therefore they were not being the church Jesus promised to build.

The same is true today. Many Christians don't understand the church and therefore are not really living as the church. For many, the church is something they attend - with very few ramifications other than that. As we conclude this study in which we have been exploring what it means to truly be the church, I want us to examine the three metaphors Paul gives us in this Ephesians passage. In many ways these three pictures Paul gives us of the church are a fitting summary of this entire book and a good place to finish.

> *Consequently, you are no longer foreigners and aliens, but fellow citizens with God's people and members of God's household. (Ephesians 2:19)*

The first metaphor Paul uses is that of citizens in the kingdom of heaven (or kingdom of God). He says, *"you are no longer foreigners and aliens."* Foreigners and aliens were often looked at with suspicion and discriminated against and this is how the Gentiles were treated before Christ established the church. They were like second-class citizens as far as worshiping God was concerned. They could not enter the temple; they could not be priests and, in most cases, were despised by Israel.

However, in Christ, Gentile Christians were now full citizens of God's kingdom. Among Christians there is disagreement over what the kingdom of heaven is. John the Baptist preached about the kingdom of heaven a lot and so did Christ and His apostles (cf. Matt 3:2, 10:7). However, in studying texts on the kingdom of heaven, it clearly has both a present and a future reality. For example, this one from Luke:

> *Once, on being asked by the Pharisees when the kingdom of God would come, Jesus replied, "The coming of the kingdom of God is not something that can be observed, nor will people say, 'Here it is,' or 'There it is,' because the kingdom of God is in your midst."* (Luke 17:20-21)

Christ says the kingdom of God is within you, or this can be translated *"in your midst."* The kingdom of heaven is present, and yet, we still wait for its complete fulfilment. In the Lord's Prayer, we pray, *"Your kingdom come. Your will be done in earth, as it is in heaven"* (Matthew 6:10). Therefore, you could say the kingdom of heaven is wherever people proclaim submission to God. It is in our hearts, and yet it is also a coming reality. One day, at Christ's coming, He will literally rule on this earth as in heaven and as the church, we should currently live as citizens of this kingdom. How does that look?

1. *Heavenly citizens will have different cultural norms than those of the earth.*

These different cultural norms include different speech, dress, values, etc. Ephesians 4:29 says, *"Do not let any unwholesome talk come out of your mouths, but only what is helpful for building others up according to their needs, that it may benefit those who listen."* Citizens of heaven will only let words come out of their mouths that will be helpful and build others up. They will not be known for sexual jokes, swearing, or other language that defiles.

1 Timothy 2:9 says, *"I also want women to dress modestly, with decency and propriety, not with braided hair or gold or pearls or expensive clothes."* Though Paul speaks to women in this text, the principles apply to all Christians. In the world clothes are often

used to show one's wealth and to draw attention and glory to the wearer. But the Christian will want all glory to go to God and therefore avoid lavish, sexually alluring, or ragged clothing (often another way of seeking attention). Not only will Christians be different in their talk and their appearance, but also in the way they think.

In Romans 12:2 Paul says, *"Do not conform to the pattern of this world but be transformed by the renewing of your mind."* The world culture trains people how to think about beauty, success, life, and death. Citizens of the kingdom of heaven will think very differently about these things because their views are based on Scripture. Citizens of heaven will be continually transforming their minds through the Word of God.

2. Heavenly citizens will continually walk in righteousness.

Romans 14:17 says, *"For the kingdom of God is not a matter of eating and drinking, but of righteousness, peace and joy in the Holy Spirit."* These are all present realities that should be growing in our lives. We are meant to be manifesting the righteousness of Christ in our lives more and more and helping others to do so as well. We will be living in the reality of our peace with God which leads to peace with others. We will also be growing in joy regardless of our circumstances because our joy is always in God. *"Rejoice in the Lord, again I say, 'Rejoice!"* (Philippians 4:4)

3. Heavenly citizens will continually proclaim the kingdom to others.

Acts 28:31 says this about Paul: *"He proclaimed the kingdom of God and taught about the Lord Jesus Christ — with all boldness and without hindrance!"* Paul continually proclaimed the kingdom of God - preaching the gospel of Jesus Christ. This should be true for us as well. As citizens of heaven, we should continually proclaim the gospel to all who will hear. The good news is that life in this present world is not the best there is - there is more. The sin, discord, death, and decay of this world are not God's plan for us. God has more. Jesus Christ ushered in a whole new world – a new kingdom – into which He calls each of us.

4. *Heavenly citizens will long for the kingdom of heaven.*

Hebrews 11:16 says this about Abraham and the other patriarchs of the faith: *"Instead, they were longing for a better country - a heavenly one. Therefore, God is not ashamed to be called their God, for he has prepared a city for them."*

Though living on the earth, Abraham and the patriarchs longed for their heavenly home - and God is not ashamed to be called their God. God is pleased with those who long for the coming kingdom.

One of the ways we do this is by praying for it. Again, the Lord's Prayer gives us those mighty words, *"Your kingdom come. Your will be done."* We should long for it especially as we see the sin and destruction happening daily in our world. Another way we long for the kingdom is by longing for our King - our Saviour - to come. Paul says this in

> *But our citizenship is in heaven. And we eagerly await a Saviour from there, the Lord Jesus Christ, who, by the power that enables him to bring everything under his control, will transform our lowly bodies so that they will be like his glorious body.* (Philippians 3:20-21)

If we are truly being the church, then we will be living as citizens of the kingdom of heaven. Our language, our behaviour, our priorities and our hopes will be different to the world around us. The next way that Christians can be the church is by living as family members.

> *Consequently, you are no longer foreigners and aliens, but fellow citizens with God's people and members of God's household.* (Ephesians 2:19)

Not only has Christ made us heavenly citizens, but also members of the same family. There is greater unity and intimacy between family members than between citizens. This should be something that characterizes Christians. Christ says this about His followers:

> *"Who is my mother, and who are my brothers?" Pointing to his disciples, he said, "Here are my mother and my brothers. For whoever does the will of my Father in heaven is my brother and sister and mother. (Matthew 12:48-50)*

Christ regarded His disciples as family members and God as their Father. He taught the disciples to pray, *"Our Father, who is in heaven, hallowed be Your name ..."* (Matthew 6:9). When we began following Christ, we became family. This family includes people from different socio-economic backgrounds, races, ethnic groups and it includes believers both in heaven and here on earth. Ephesians 3:14-15 says, *"For this reason I kneel before the Father, from whom his whole family in heaven and on earth derives its name."*

In 1 Timothy 5:1-2, Paul says this about how believers should treat one another: *"Do not rebuke an older man harshly but exhort him as if he were your father. Treat younger men as brothers, older women as mothers, and younger women as sisters, with absolute purity."* We should treat one another as family. Christ said, *"They will know you are my disciples by the way you love one another."* (John 13:35). We are to be known by this intimate familial love.

1. *As family, believers often use familial terms.*

Paul calls Timothy his *"son in the faith"* (1 Timothy 1:2). He refers to himself as a *"father"* to the Corinthians (1 Corinthians 4:15) and calls the Romans *"brothers and sisters"* (Romans 12:1). We should feel comfortable using these familial terms as well.

2. *As family, believers place a high priority on being the church.*

Galatians 6:10 says, *"Therefore, as we have opportunity, let us do good to all people, especially to those who belong to the family of believers."* Yes, we should do good to all, but especially to fellow believers. They should be our priority. When something is your priority, you invest your time, money, and energy in it, and you give up other things to focus on it. This should be true of our investment in the Body of Christ.

Sadly, for too many people, job, schooling and housing are the main priorities instead of the church. Believers often uproot their families from a great church community where God is using them and move for career and other opportunities. This often leads to spiritual struggles. They find a new fellowship of believers, but often struggle to get involved - and it never feels like home. Their spiritual life suffers because they didn't prioritize their kingdom ministry - their Christian family. Where has God planted you? How is God calling you to make church and the mission of Christ your priority?

3. *As family, believers must develop intimate relationships with one another.*

Family is a place where we share intimate secrets and struggles, and this should be true of the church as well. James 5:16 says, *"Therefore confess your sins to each other and pray for each other so that you may be healed. The prayer of a righteous man is powerful and effective."*

Sadly, many people have no transparency in their church relationships. People in the church are too often kept at arm's length, if not an entire body's length! We need to develop close relationships within the body of Christ. We should learn to confess our sins and share our successes with one another and also to seek the prayers of the saints. These are practical aspects of being family and being the church.

4. *As family, believers must encourage one another in their spiritual growth.*

In families, parents invest their lives, money, and time in helping their children grow as individuals. Church members should help one another grow as well, especially in their relationship with Christ. This is the priority of people who are being the church. As the writer of Hebrews says,

> *"And let us consider how we may spur one another on toward love and good deeds."* (Hebrews 10:24).

Paul also teaches that the Gentiles are being built into a holy temple where God dwells.

> *.. built on the foundation of the apostles and prophets, with Christ Jesus himself as the chief cornerstone. In him the whole building is joined together and rises to become a holy temple in the Lord. And in him you too are being built together to become a dwelling in which God lives by his Spirit. (Ephesians 2:20-22)*

No doubt this conjured up images of the Jewish temple, which Gentiles could never fully enter. However, they were now God's temple.

1. *As God's temple, we will constantly worship God.*

That was the primary purpose of the physical temple. There, people gathered to worship and offer sacrifices pleasing to God. Hebrews 13:15-16 says: *"Through Jesus, therefore, let us continually offer to God a sacrifice of praise - the fruit of lips that confess his name. And do not forget to do good and to share with others, for with such sacrifices God is pleased."* Here the author says praise, good works, and giving are sacrifices that please God. This will be our continual endeavour as God's temple. We will ask ourselves daily, *"How can I worship and bless God today both individually and with other believers?"*

Paul also tells us in 1 Corinthians 10:31, *"So whether you eat or drink or whatever you do, do it all for the glory of God."* Everything we do can and should be worship.

2. *As God's temple, we will live carefully - in a God-honouring manner.*

In one of Watchman Nee's books he says that if you have a little bit of change in your pocket, you can walk around carefree. However, if you have a large sum of money in your pocket, you will walk very carefully, lest you lose it. Not that we can lose God, but he who dwells in us is so valuable that His indwelling should drastically change how we walk, how we think and how we live. Everything should be different.

So let us walk carefully so we might always honour God with our mouths and our meditations. Let us always remember that our individual bodies, and also, we as the church, are his temple – the dwelling place of God.

3. *As God's temple, we will live as God's holy people*

The priests and Levites made sure that God's temple was never defiled. There were ceremonial washings and cleansings even for the plates in the temple. In the same way, as the temple of God, we will keep ourselves from anything that might defile. In 1 Thessalonians 5:22 Paul says, *"Avoid every kind of evil."* When Jesus went into the temple, He made a whip and turned over tables because God's house was being defiled. We must have that same type of zeal for God's temple - our bodies and the church. We must get rid of all sin and anything that does not honour God. Paul further expands on this idea of God's temple when he reminds us of three critical elements.

(a) *The apostles and prophets are the foundation of the temple*

Ephesians 2:20 says the temple is built on the *"foundation of the apostles and prophets."* There is some controversy over this. Is Paul referring to the Old Testament prophets and the New Testament apostles? Or is he referring to New Testament apostles and prophets? It's likely he is referring only to those who ministered in the New Testament era. The primary support for this view is the order in which he lists the two groups. If he is referring to the Old Testament prophets, then it would make sense that the prophets would be listed first. Instead, he is probably referring to those who joined with the apostles in building the church.

> *In reading this, then, you will be able to understand my insight into the mystery of Christ, which was not made known to men in other generations as it has now been revealed by the Spirit to God's holy apostles and prophets. (Ephesians 3:4-5)*

The apostles were specifically a group whom Jesus chose, called and authorized to teach in His name and who were eyewitnesses of His resurrection, consisting of the Twelve plus Paul and James and perhaps one or two others. How are the apostles and prophets the foundation of the church, especially since Scripture says Christ is the foundation of the church (1 Cor. 3:11)? The primary way the apostles and the prophets are the foundation of the church is through their teaching. They wrote what became the New Testament on which the church stands theologically and they founded local churches based on these truths. Paul confirms that here:

> By the grace God has given me, I laid a foundation as an expert builder, and someone else is building on it. But each one should be careful how he builds. For no one can lay any foundation other than the one already laid, which is Jesus Christ. (1 Cor. 3:10-11)

The apostles and prophets laid the foundation of the church through their teachings, and their emphasis on the resurrected Christ. There are several principles that we can learn from this about being the church. Since the church is built on the apostolic teaching, we, as committed members of the church, will be devoted to the apostolic teaching. As we saw in a previous chapter, the early disciples of Jesus, *"devoted themselves to the apostles' teaching and to the fellowship, to the breaking of bread and to prayer."* (Acts 2:42).

We must be devoted to daily studying the Bible, memorizing it, teaching it, and sharing it with others. Since the church is built on apostolic teaching, when seeking a church fellowship, we should also look for one that faithfully preaches the Word of God. Many church communities no longer preach from the Bible. They say it is too antiquated, full of errors, and irrelevant to the needs of the people. Instead, they preach psychology, history, tell stories, and share anecdotal socio-political diatribe. Paul warned Timothy of such a time as this:

> *"For the time will come when men will not put up with sound doctrine. Instead, to suit their own desires, they will gather around them a great number of teachers to say what their itching ears want to hear. They will turn their ears away from the truth and turn aside to myths."* (2 Timothy 4:3-4)

Because Satan knows that the Word of God is the foundation of the church, he always attacks it in his attempts to bring us down. Even at the beginning of time, Satan attacked the Word of God. He asked Eve, *"Is that really what God said?"* Tragically, that same question is being asked by a growing number of modern 'Christians' about some of the foundational truths of the Bible.

(b) Christ is the cornerstone of the temple

Ephesians 2:20-21 tells us the church is: *"built on the foundation of the apostles and prophets, with Christ Jesus himself as the chief cornerstone. In him the whole building is joined together and rises to become a holy temple in the Lord."* The cornerstone was a messianic picture of Christ in the Old Testament. Isaiah 28:16 says, *"So this is what the Sovereign LORD says: 'See, I lay a stone in Zion, a tested stone, a precious cornerstone for a sure foundation; the one who trusts will never be dismayed."*

A cornerstone was important for two reasons. It was part of the foundation, and it also fixed the angle of the building and became the standard from which the architect traced the walls and arches throughout. Since Christ is the cornerstone of the church, it is on Him, His Word and His finished work that the church is built. When Jesus asked Peter, *"Who do you say that I am,"* Peter replied, *"You are the Christ, the Son of the living God."* And Jesus replied, *"On this rock, I will build my church"* (Matthew 16:16-18). Christ is this rock. He is the cornerstone on which the church is built. Only those who accept Christ and His teachings are part of the church. Is your life built on Christ - His life, death, resurrection, and teaching? Any other foundation will fail.

Since Christ is the cornerstone of the church, it is through Him that the church is unified. Paul says this in Ephesians 2:21, *"In Him the whole building is joined together."* Then in Ephesians 2:14, *"For He Himself is our peace, Who has made the two one."* He is the one Who joins the Jews and Gentiles together, abolishing that ancient hostility. Jesus is also the One Who brings the church together today. We can only be unified because of Him, whether we are Jew, Gentile, rich, poor, male, or female. We can only have this kind of unity based on Christ. If our unity is based on culture, affinity, gender, socio-economic status, hobbies or anything else, it will not stand. Only Christ can unify the church and keep it unified. Are you walking in unity with the rest of the church? Yes, certain people's personalities may get on your nerves; they may think differently than you; they may even hurt you. However, you can seek unity because of Christ - He is the unifier. Let that commonality trump any other differences. Christ is our cornerstone.

Since Christ is the cornerstone of the church, it is through Him that we grow. Ephesians 2:21 says, *"In him the whole building is joined together and rises to become a holy temple in the Lord."* It was upon that foundation, that cornerstone, the rest of the building was constructed. In the same way, both our individual and our corporate spiritual growth come through Christ. Christ says, *"I am the vine; you are the branches. If a man remains in me and I in him, he will bear much fruit; apart from me you can do nothing"* (John 15:5).

It is only by abiding in Christ, our cornerstone, that we can grow and ultimately fulfill our purpose. We abide in Christ and therefore grow spiritually through the study of Scripture, prayer, fellowship with other believers, and serving. Many people are not growing because they are not abiding in Christ - they are not staying connected to the cornerstone.

c.   The people of God are bricks in the temple

Now the third aspect of the temple that Paul refers to is us. Ephesians 2:22 says, *"And in him you too are being built together to become a dwelling in which God lives by his Spirit."* Though Paul does not actually say so, the implication is that he is referring to individual believers as bricks or stones in the temple of God.

Peter uses this same analogy in 1 Peter 2:5 when he says, *"you also, like living stones, are being built into a spiritual house to be a holy priesthood, offering spiritual sacrifices acceptable to God through Jesus Christ."* Yes, Scripture teaches that individual believers are the temple of God. 1 Corinthians 6:19-20 says, *"Do you not know that your body is a temple of the Holy Spirit, who is in you, whom you have received from God? You are not your own; you were bought at a price. Therefore, honour God with your body."*

Scripture also teaches that when believers gather together, God is with us. 1 Corinthians 3:16 says, *"Don't you know that you yourselves are God's temple and that God's Spirit lives in you?"* The word *you* in this passage is actually plural, referring to the church. Similarly, Christ says in Matthew 18:20, *"For where two or three come together in my name, there am I with them."* When believers are present together there is a special way in which God meets with them. In fact, there are some things God does in a corporate gathering that He does not do when we are alone.

Now as 'bricks' in the 'temple of God' we obviously need one another. A brick is not good for much by itself. But when it is bound together with other bricks, it becomes part of a beautiful building. In the same way, apart from the body of Christ, we may miss God's best. As bricks in the temple of God, the Lord is constantly adding other bricks until the temple is complete, and we must aid in that process. One day God will add the final Jews and Gentiles to the church and the 'temple' will be finished. He has called us to partner with Him in that process by faithfully sharing the gospel with others.

In Matthew 28:19 we are called and commissioned to, *"go throughout the earth and make disciples of all nations."* The disciples are the bricks Jesus uses to build His church and that church which Jesus promised to build is the only church God recognises, empowers and trusts to fulfil His Kingdom plan and purpose.

As I draw this book to a close, I don't believe for a moment that I have said all that could be said about what it means to truly be the church. I could probably write another book now as I continue to explore the depth and breadth of this wonderful faith community into which God has called each of us. However, I do sincerely believe that if you understand, embrace and apply the teaching in this book, Jesus will fulfill His promise to build His church in you, through you and around you.

You will marvel at what is possible as you fully embrace the church that God sees and longs for, which may not be the church humans have tried to build in Jesus' name.

You will be amazed at what God can achieve through you and the believers around you when you decide you want to stop just going to church and start being the church! But we need to work with God here and go looking for His hand at work and listen for His voice to us. Each chapter in this book needs be studied and prayed through - not just read once and discarded. I would strongly suggest when you have made your way to the end of this book, that you go back and work through it all again, soaked in prayer, as you ask God to reveal His word to you. If you choose to spend that time and let God really drive His truths home in your heart, then I can guarantee that 'being the church' will not be a chore, an expectation or a religious activity - it will be a spontaneous reality as the life of Christ explodes within you.

Then, before we know it, the book of Acts will no longer be a dusty historical account of where this all began, it will once again be a commentary on where we are now, and who we are becoming as we give the church back to God, give the ministry back to God's people, and watch the Lord do today what He did back in the beginning. That is my only agenda. That is the reason I preach and teach and write: I want to lead people to the God Who still speaks, still heals, still transforms lives and whole communities. Everything I do, say, preach, write and pray is directed towards that end.

I truly believe God is always ready to redeem what we've lost and give us the only thing we ever truly needed: Jesus – the living, present, Lord of the church and the One Who promised to build His church, right here, right now, if we let go the reigns and trust Him.

www.ingramcontent.com/pod-product-compliance
Lightning Source LLC
Chambersburg PA
CBHW051434290426
44109CB00016B/1555